Dictations
for
Discussion

A Listening/Speaking Text

Judy DeFilippo
Catherine Sadow

PRO LINGUA ASSOCIATES

Pro Lingua Associates, Publishers
P.O. Box 1348
Brattleboro, Vermont 05302 USA
Office: 802 257 7779
Orders: 800 366 4775
Email: info@ProLinguaAssociates.com
WebStore www.ProLinguaAssociates.com
SAN: 216-0579

*At **Pro Lingua***
our objective is to foster an approach
to learning and teaching that we call
***interplay,** the **inter**action of language*
learners and teachers with their materials,
with the language and culture,
and with each other in active,
creative, and productive
play.

Copyright © 2003 by Judy DeFilippo and Catherine Sadow
For a listing of other materials under copyright, see the acknowledgements on page v.

ISBN 0-86647-167-7

Dictations for Discussion was designed by Arthur A. Burrows. It was set in Palatino, the most widely used, and pirated, face of the twentieth century which was designed by Hermann Zapf in 1948 in Frankfurt. Although modern, it is based on Renaissance designs typical of the Palatinate area in Germany. The clipart illustrating the book is from *The Big Box of Art,* Copyright © 2001 Hemera Technologies Inc., and *Art Explosion 750,000 Images,* Copyright © 1995-2000 Nova Development Corporation. The book was printed and bound by Capital City Press in Montpelier, Vermont.

Printed in the United States of America
First printing 2003. 2000 copies in print.

Contents

Acknowledgements

The authors based many of their activities on concepts introduced by P. Davis and M. Rinvolucri, who co-authored ***Dictation, New Methods, New Possibilities,*** Cambridge University Press, 1988.

The authors are grateful to the authors, publishers, and others who have given permission to reprint copyrighted materials:

American Psychological Association: *Sexual Orientation*

The Associated Press: *Marriage* and *Staying in the Nest*

The Boston Globe

    Photo of Dogs, Paul Baker

    Men Putting Family First, Diane E. Lewis

    Concerns Over Increasing U.S. Birthweights, Douglas Bekin

    As U.S. Obesity Rises, Karen Hsu

    Deep Pockets Are In, Cindy Rodriguez

    Older Learner's Graduation an Inspiration, Victoria Benning

    Lucky Dishes for New Year, Bonnie Tsui

    Three Little Words by Erma Bombeck; The Aaron Priest Literary Agency

    Obituary of Ruth Rothfarb, Tom Long

    Eating Smart, Jean Kressy

    Back to School Shocking, Laura Pappano

    Clone Research, Raja Mishra

Center for Counseling and Student Development at Northeastern University: *Facts on Drinking*

Creators Syndicate: Ann Landers Permission

David Muir and Pressman Toys: cards from *Judge for Yourself*

The Economist: *A World Empire by Other Means*

The Internet: *How's Your Mental Health?* AskpsychMD.com by Mark Faber, MD

    Learning Styles

    Open Adoption, Bill and Eve Kuhlemeier Website

The New York Times: *Stroked, Poked, and Hypnotized* by D. Wilkinson; *Hold the Pickles–Hold the Lettuce* by M. Kakutani

The Northeastern News: *Trials of Tipping; Smokers' Rights; So Whattcha Speakin'*

Oceana Publications, Inc.: *Election Day* by M. B. Lorenz

The Patriot Ledger: *Cheating* by Dina Gerdeman; *There's No Purr-fect Answer* by D. Conkey

Random House, Inc.: Selection from *Palace of Desire* by Naguib Mafouz

Sage Publications: *The Immaculate Americans* by Jack Levin

Simon and Schuster: *The Psychology of Shopping* by Paco Underhill

USA Today: *Answering the Need to Help* by Perry Flicker

Workman Publishers: *What Would You Do If ...?; Golden Wedding Anniversary; Workplace Ethics*

In memory of
Edgar Sather

Introduction

Dictations for Discussion is an intermediate to advanced level text that is intended to improve the listening and speaking skills of ESL students. Of course, since skills are not isolated from each other, reading and writing are also reinforced, along with progress in vocabulary and grammar This text provides a wide variety of dictations from authentic materials that include provocative news items, problems to solve, and decisions to make. Each dictation naturally leads to a discussion activity that can take ten, twenty, or thirty minutes.

The dictation/discussion units may be used in any order, depending on the needs, interests, and levels of the students. The units are classified into six topic areas, but one topic is not necessarily easier or harder than another. Each unit is labeled at the top of every page with proficiency indicators, as follows:

I = Intermediate
H = High Intermediate
A = Advanced

❀ Types of Dictation ❀

Dictation has been presented in many forms through the years in reading, listening, grammar, and writing classes. It is also used as an assessment procedure. This text, however, does not deal with scoring or analyzing student work. It is meant to be a challenging and open springboard to discussion in which students are encouraged to use the language they have just learned. In this text there are four types of dictation, described below.

Partial (sometimes known as *cloze*)

Most of the dictations in this text are partial dictations where words, phrases, or chunks of language have been deleted and students are required to listen and write down the missing words. All the dictations should be discussed upon completion, and pair work is encouraged here.

Pair (sometimes known as *mutual*)

This dictation requires students to work in pairs to combine two-part texts into one continuous piece. One student has a copy of dictation Part A, and the other has dictation Part B. Each student has half of the text. They should not look at each other's sheets. Student A dictates and B writes, then B dictates and A writes, and so on until the story is complete.

Dictogloss

This form of dictation is an excellent way to develop a connection between what the learner hears and the written language. In this listening/speaking text, however, the focus is on getting the gist or main idea of a sentence or short paragraph and preparing students to take notes.

There are many variations of the dictogloss technique. In the directions for the sentence level dictogloss, students are told that they will hear a sentence only once, after which they are to jot down the words they can recall and try to reconstruct the sentence in writing as accurately as they can. The first time this is done, the teacher will probably have to allow the students a second reading until they discover that they need to pay attention the first time around. As the students work at rebuilding the sentence, they can work in pairs and then fours. For intermediate level students, the length of the sentence dictated should be about 12-15 words, whereas for higher level students the sentence can be up to 25 words.

Also included are very short paragraphs to be dictated. In this kind of dictation, the students should focus more on the meaning of the paragraph than on the individual sentences; they are not expected to get everything word for word. The teacher may read each paragraph once at normal speed while the students just listen; then the teacher can read it again with longer pauses between sentences if necessary. The students write only one sentence which expresses the main idea of the entire paragraph.

Prediction

Prediction lessons come in two parts. The first part focuses more on reading skills and grammar. The students are required to work in pairs, read the passage, and predict (or guess) what is in each blank space. Any logical or grammatically correct word or phrase can be accepted. Part Two requires the students to listen to the same passage and see if their guesses were correct, or similar.

❀ Tips for Teachers ❀

1. When reading the dictations, try to speak naturally, at normal speed, keeping the features of the spoken language. If you are reading the text from the appendix at normal speed and you know the exercise will be fairly easy for your students, give the word, phrase, or chunk of language only once. Try to start with a pace that is comfortable for your students and then make them work a bit at understanding. If you think the text will be difficult for the students, repeat two, possibly three times. It's up to you to decide what works best. If you have to repeat more than three times, the text is too difficult for the students.

2. The students may want to check the spelling of a word or words as you are giving the dictation. It's best to tell them to wait until the end of the activity.

3. For numbers, have the students write numerals, rather than the word (15, instead of *fifteen*), except for single digit numbers (1-9). They should also use dollar ($) and percentage symbols (%), rather than writing out the words.

4. One key to making the dictation a positive experience is to have students correct their own work. When the dictation is completed, the students check with each other in pairs on what they've heard as you walk around helping and clarifying. This, in itself, allows for a great deal of discussion. After they have self-corrected, they can turn to the full dictation texts for confirmation. You can then go over the dictation with the class and discuss whatever vocabulary or concepts they don't understand.

5. Rather than read the dictations from the appendix, you may find it helpful to copy the page you're dictating and fill in the blanks yourself ahead of time. This is helpful when giving feedback. It's easier when you're working from the same page as your students. Here is an example:

Cheating in the classroom isn't just about *copying* someone's paper or writing answers on a *crib sheet*. With the *internet*, cheating has gone *high tech*.

6. There was no pattern that was followed when choosing words or phrases to be deleted. Sometimes the deletions focus on idioms, sometimes on numbers, sometimes grammar, sometimes vocabulary.

7. *Dictations for Discussion* also works well for substitute teachers, since a minimum amount of preparation is needed.

8. You and your students can also create dictations from local newspapers, the internet, or any other source. This way you can choose a timely topic and easily adapt it to the level of your students.

9. With more advanced students, you may want to ask a student to give a dictation by reading from the appendix. The reader may prepare for this by listening to the CD.

10. **Discussions.** The discussions can be done by pairs, small groups, or the entire class. As the students finish discussing each question, they can check it off in the space after the number. Doing this can ensure that the topic is fully and carefully discussed. When dealing with sensitive or controversial topics, it's important to be sure that the class atmosphere is an open one where your students can express themselves and know that their opinions will be respected and welcomed. If you have misgivings about a particular topic, don't do it!

❀ Using a Listening Laboratory ❀

A Compact Disc is available for use in class or in a language laboratory. Almost any dictation that is done in class can also be done in the language lab. However, there are some additional things that can be done in the lab that cannot be done in the classroom.

1. You can read a short partial dictation in the lab, and then have the students read what they have written onto their tapes. You can collect both and then on the student tape give some feedback on their pronunciation.

2. The students create their own partial dictation and make four or five copies of it. They read it carefully onto their tape and leave the tapes at their stations. They then move from station to station doing each other's dictations. This assignment can follow a general theme, or it can be a specific item such as a joke or poem.

3. Dictate a chunk of language. The student listens and records it on tape. Add another chunk. The student records again. At the end of the short, fairly simple dictation, the student rewinds the tape and transcribes it. Once again, collect the tape and paper and make appropriate comments and corrections on the tape.

4. Dictate a problem. An example might be a "Dear Abby" that you have turned into a dictation. After each student has done the dictation, they talk on their tape about their solution to the problem. You can collect the tape, and respond on it to their solution, or the students can move from station to station listening to their fellow students and making comments of agreement or disagreement onto their classmates' tapes. By preparing short, easy-to-understand dictations first, you can also use this technique to introduce current political or social topics that you think will be of particular interest to the students.

On the Compact Disc, each of the full dictation texts is on a separate track. In this text, the CD track numbers are given in the table of contents (iii-iv). They are also given next to the titles of the gapped texts on which the students take their dictations and next to the titles of the full dictation texts in the appendix.

❀ Full Dictation Texts ❀

The appendix at the back of the book starting on page 125 includes the complete texts of the dictations. You or a student can give dictations by reading these. However, it is important for students to hear different voices, so you may want to use the CD from time to time.

Dictations
for
Discussion

Immigration Statistics

dictation on page 127 (CD 1 TRACK 1)

Introduction

Recent Census Bureau reports indicate that immigration to the United States has reached new peaks. One in five Americans was either born in a foreign country or has a parent who was born overseas. With the present population at 280,000,000 you can calculate the number of foreign-born living in the U.S. Discuss with your class the main reasons people immigrate to another country.

Dictation ✿ *Write the correct word or number in the blank space. Correct and discuss the dictation.*

Here are some recent immigration statistics. INS stands for Immigration and Naturalization Service.

1. Since the founding of the U.S., more than _____ _____ from every _____ have settled here.

2. _____ _____ _____, an average of more than _____ immigrants, legal and _____, settled in the U.S. each year.

3. Legal immigration _____ between _____ and _____ each year, and the INS estimates that _____ _____ _____ settle here each year.

4. _____ _____, more than _____ immigrants have settled here, representing about _____ – _____ of all people _____ _____ _____.

5. The largest number of legal immigrants to come in the _____ and _____ came from _____, Cambodia, Laos, Mexico, El Salvador, Guatemala, and Haiti.

6. Of the immigrant groups, there are _____ Latinos, now the _____ minority, _____ _____ – _____.

7. In California, home to over _____ Asian-Americans, _____% of all Californians are working for _____ – _____ businesses or paying rent to an Asian _____.

Discussion ✿ *Discuss these questions with a partner. Share your ideas with the class.*

1. ____ What groups of immigrants can be found in your country?

2. ____ What kind of work can they find?

3. ____ Do they suffer from discrimination? If yes, in what ways?

4. ____ Can they become citizens? How long does it take to become one?

5. ____ Do they eventually return home? Why or why not?

Men Putting Family First *page 128 (CD 1 TRACK 2)*

Introduction

In recent years men have been taking a more active role in parenting, and enjoying it! With a partner, look at the following five statements about parenting. If you strongly agree, put a +2, if you agree, put +1, if you have no opinion put 0. If you disagree, put –1 and strongly disagree, put –2. Share your opinions with a partner or the class.

_____ 1. Married women with small children should not work outside the home.

_____ 2. Married couples who choose not to have children are selfish.

_____ 3. A father is as important as a mother in raising young children.

_____ 4. Men's priorities should be their jobs and their careers.

_____ 5. Equality between husbands and wives is one of the main causes of divorce.

Dictation ❧ *Write the correct word in the blank space. Correct and discuss the dictation.*

While previous studies _____ American men as more _____ _____ power, prestige, or money than about their families, _____ _____ from The Radcliffe Public Policy Center indicate men between the ages of _____ _____ _____ are more likely to _____ _____ _____ _____.

In releasing its _____ _____ of attitudes about work, life, and family relationships, Radcliffe said the findings suggest a _____ _____, with younger men _____ _____ with their fathers and grandfathers.

The study involved phone interviews with _____ men and _____ women. The _____ _____ _____ is plus or minus _____ percentage points.

Of the male participants between ages twenty and _____, about_____% placed time with family at the top of a wish list that included _____ _____. Additionally, _____% said they would give up a portion of their pay _____ _____ they could have more time with their families. In contrast, _____% of the men between _____ and_____ said doing work that allowed them to _____ _____ _____ was more important than community service, additional family time, or _____ _____. Of men _____ _____ _____ _____, _____% said they were chiefly concerned with developing good relations _____ _____.

"The men who are in their _____ have always seen themselves as _____

_____," said Paula Rayman, director of the Radcliffe Center. "If you look at the

_____ _____ over the years, you'll find that the _____ _____

in their _____ _____ _____ grew up thinking of themselves as _____

_____. Younger men, however, are working _____ _____, and

they are more likely to talk about sharing family responsibilities and _____ _____."

When Harris _____ interviewed women ages _____ _____ _____, they

pinpointed _____ _____ : _____% said they did not plan to have any children,

up from _____% in a _____ survey. "These are young women with _____ _____

_____ or people with single parents who now feel that it's impossible _____ _____

_____ _____,"Rayman said. These young women are not saying they are not going to

get married, but they are _____ _____ having children. And what we are seeing is

that the average age for women to have children _____ _____ _____

_____ years old to approximately _____ years old, a _____ – _____ _____

for the first child.

Discussion ❀ *Discuss these questions with a partner. Share your ideas with the class.*

1. ____ Is this information surprising to you? Why or why not?

2. ____ Do you see any similar cultural trends in your country? Explain.

3. ____ Do you think there are some fathers who do a better job of parenting than mothers?

4. ____ Under what circumstances could you see the father being the "househusband"
either temporarily or permanently?

5. ____ If a wife made a lot more money than her husband, would that be an issue for:
        a. you?   b. a newly-married couple?
        c. a couple married 25 years?   d. your parents?

6. ____ When women say it is impossible "to do it all," what do they mean?

7. ____ How do you see your role as a parent?

Staying in the Nest *page 129 (CD 1 TRACK 3)*

Introduction

Ward Simpson, father of three grown children, says, "Most parents complain that their kids never visit them, but mine never leave." "Boomerang Kids" is the name coined by the media to describe young adults who leave home to attend college or to work away from home, but decide for various reasons to return home to live with their parents. Before doing the dictation, discuss the meaning of baby boomers and boomerang.

Dictation ❀ *Write the correct word or number in the blank space. Correct and discuss the dictation.*

The caps and gowns have been used and returned, yet many Baby Boomers are finding _____ _____ _____ to their grown-up kids' life away from home has been _____ _____ indefinitely.

In a development that _____ _____ _____ many boomers in the generation-gap days of _____ _____ _____, returning to the nest — or_____ _____ it — is becoming increasingly commonplace. A _____ _____ and _____ _____ _____ appear to have accelerated the trend and produced more of what American Demographics magazine calls "_____."

This year, about _____ or _____% of university graduates plan to live _____ _____ _____ for some period of time. Sociologists and other observers say that besides the _____ _____, boomers themselves – those turning _____ to _____ this year – are _____ _____ _____.

"The negative thing about moving home has really _____ _____," says author Faith Popcorn. "A lot of parents have a _____ – _____ _____ with their kids. I think _____ _____ parents really have gotten the idea that home is _____ _____ _____, and they never wanted their kids to leave _____ _____ _____ _____."

The financial security of the most _____ _____ _____ and their bigger houses have made this _____ – _____ living arrangement much more appealing _____ _____ _____. Ward Simpson and his wife have two sons and a daughter _____ _____ _____ _____ and coming back, going away and moving back. "_____ _____ _____ that their children never visit them but mine never leave – and I _____ _____ _____ _____ _____."

The _____ _____ trend first emerged in the 1980s before _____ _____ in the 1990s. Now it is on the increase again following the _____ – _____ _____ and with the first _____ of Baby Boomers' _____ million children _____ _____.

The trend _____ _____ when boom times return, but it looks _____ _____ _____ _____. The U.S. Census shows _____ million Americans ages _____ to _____ live with their parents – a group now _____ _____ from marketers because it has lots of disposable income and _____ _____ _____.

Discussion ❀ *Discuss these questions with a partner. Share your ideas with the class.*

1. ____ What are the advantages and disadvantages of living at home after graduation from a university?

2. ____ Is this trend to "stay in the nest" happening in your country as well?

3. ____ Is it easier for men to "stay in the nest" than it is for women? Do men have more freedom?

4. ____ Is the relationship between parents and children in your country the same as it was a generation ago? Explain.

5. ____ This article indicates that the American relationship between parents and children has changed. Do you think this is a positive or negative change?

6. ____ Is it customary for you to live near your parents after you leave school or after you marry?

7. ____ Should college graduates who have a good job, and live at home, pay their parents any "rent" or give money to help them pay the bills?

8. ____ Considering the advantages and disadvantages of staying in the nest or having your own place, which would you prefer? Why?

Marriage and Divorce *page 130 (CD 1 TRACK 4)*

Introduction

The U.S. Census Bureau recently issued a marriage and divorce report after studying the data and interviewing 37,000 Americans. While most Americans are not surprised to hear that nearly half of first marriages end in divorce, it's interesting to compare those statistics to 1960 when only one in three marriages ended in divorce. Here are some other observations.

Dictation ❀ *Write the correct word or number in the blank space. Correct and discuss the dictation.*

1. People with a college degree _____ _____ _____ _____ and stay married.

2. Among married women ages 25 to _____ with a college degree, 15 _____ _____ _____ divorced within a year, compared with _____ out of 1000 women with just a _____ _____ _____ .

3. The average age of a first marriage _____ to _____ years for women and _____ for men.

4. In the 1950s and 1960s the _____ _____ for women to marry was _____ and for men it was _____ .

5. Divorce is least likely to _____ among _____ and most likely to occur among _____ – _____ .

Dictogloss ❀ *Listen to a complete sentence only once and write down the words you can remember on a separate piece of paper. With a partner, try to reconstruct the entire sentence and write it below.*

1.

2.

3.

4.

5.

Discussion ❧ *Discuss these questions with a partner. Share your ideas with the class.*

1. _____ 9 out of 10 Americans are expected to marry in their lifetime. This is a big change from the 1950s, when everyone was expected to get married. What reasons can you give for this change in expectations?

2. _____ Compare the census report above with trends that you see in your country.

3. _____ Marriage is a legal contract. When couples decide to divorce they have to hire a lawyer and go to court to end the contract. Couples must come to an agreement on alimony, property settlement, and child custody and support. Lawyers are needed to settle these problems. What is the procedure in your culture? Do parents ever get joint custody of the children? (divided time between parents) Do fathers ever get custody?

4. _____ Here are some legal grounds for divorce. Which do you think are most common?

Irreconcilable differences	Money	Imprisonment
Drug addiction	Alcoholism	Certain illnesses
Desertion	Adultery	Mental/physical abuse

5. _____ Some Americans who are between the ages of 60 and 80 and who have lost a spouse decide to remarry. Discuss the advantages and disadvantages of remarrying late in life.

6. _____ Describe a typical wedding in your country.

7. _____ Are arranged marriages common in your culture?

Dictation ❧ *Write the words in the blanks, discuss the problem with a partner, and think of a resolution.*

In the following paragraph, a teenager is asking for advice.

My parents are _____. I live with my mother. I spend two _____ a month with my dad and one month in the summer with him. I love my father but he has _____, and I don't really like his new wife, Amy. My father is real nice to me and takes me places, but Amy _____ _____ _____ _____ and I feel uncomfortable around her.

Now that I'm 15, I _____ _____ spend more time at home with my friends. I also want to get a _____ – _____ job this summer. Do you think my father will be _____ if I don't visit him this summer? What do you think I should do?

Open Adoption *page 131 (CD 1 TRACK 5)*

Introduction

Open adoption is a legal process where the biological parents, called birthparents, not only choose the adoptive parents but also remain in contact with their child and his/her parents. People who select open adoption believe that it is important for the birthparents to know how their child is doing and for the child to have direct access to information and support from the birthparents. It is a unique partnership with separate and distinct roles. In the dictation you will hear an interview with a mother and father who share their experience as adoptive parents of two sons.

Dictation ❀ *Write the correct word or number in the blank space. Correct and discuss the dictation.*

Q. Why did you choose an open adoption?

A. This is a big question, but it _____ _____ _____ _____ ; once we got over

the fear that everyone seems to have at first, we _____ _____ _____ of

openness. Without the secrecy involved in traditional, _____ _____ adoption, there

will never be the questions of: "Why did my birthmom _____ _____ _____?" Or,

"I wonder _____ _____ to my baby?" Or, "_____ _____ _____ _____?"

Or, "What kind of woman _____ _____ to this child?" When there are answers

_____ _____ _____, it's better and healthier for everyone.

Q. Aren't you worried that the birthmom will want her baby back?

A. _____ _____ _____ _____ of the agency we went with, is the excellent counseling

that was provided to both us and our children's birthmoms. _____ ____ _____ of this

counseling, we were all comfortable with our _____ _____ _____.

Because of this comfort, _____ _____ _____ _____ of a reclaim situation. Also,

we knew that the agency we used followed the _____ _____ and provided for

a fairly secure relinquishment of _____ _____ _____. This was the

only way we _____ _____ _____ doing our second adoption.

Q. Are you going to maintain contact with your sons' birthmoms?

A. Yes, we have a very _____ _____ with our sons' birthmoms. We live

_____ _____ to Will's birthmom and visit _____. We have been to Will's

_____-_____ birthday party, and they came to Will's first birthday party. We _____

_____ email and cards. Our sons will always have their _____ in _____

_____, as well as another set of _____! (There's _____

_____ _____ as too many Grandmas and Grandpas!) Many people seem

to think that _____ _____ involved would _____ _____

_____ – _____or maybe a step-parent relationship. This _____ _____ _____

_____. We are the "_____ and _____" parents of our children.

Discussion ❀ _Discuss these questions with a partner. Share your ideas with the class._

1. ____ Is adoption common in your culture? Is open adoption an option? How do you feel about adoption?
2. ____ Why would a person give up a child for adoption?
3. ____ In the interview the mother mentions her son's half-sister. What does this mean?
4. ____ Adoptive parents are advised to tell their children that they are adopted as soon as they understand what adoption means. Why is this advice usually followed?

Discussion ❀ _Read the situations. Discuss the questions with a partner. Share your ideas with the class._

Situation 1: Meg Harris, who is happily married with two children, was adopted 40 years ago and has wonderful parents. But she always had questions that bothered her for many years and started a ten-month search for her birthparents. By law, any adopted child can seek biological parents. She discovered that her father had recently died and left no family. She was excited when she located her birthmother but was bitterly disappointed when her mother refused to see her. Her mother was married and hadn't told her two adult children about Meg, and didn't want them to know.

_____ Was Meg's biological mother wise not to meet with her? Why or why not?
_____ What questions do you think Meg would want to ask her biological parents?

Situation 2: In their 40 years of marriage, Carol and Bob Deering have adopted more than 25 disabled children, now ranging in ages from 10 to 33. They believe that all children deserve a loving home and they take the kids that most people don't want or can't handle. The children are Black, White, Asian, and Latino, but all have some kind of physical or mental disability. For example, they adopt children with cerebral palsy, brain damage, or Down syndrome. Many had mothers who were drug abusers. Some suffered physical abuse. In their large New York home they currently have six young adults living with them.

____What qualities do the Deerings have to have in order to deal with these children?
____Would you consider adopting a disabled child?

Three Little Words *page 133 (CD 1 TRACK 6)*

Introduction

From the time we are very small until we are adults, our parents give us advice. Sometimes, although negative, it is in positive imperative form: "Come home before midnight." Sometimes, although negative, it is in the form of a question: "Isn't that skirt too short?" Sometimes it is in direct negative imperative form: "Don't put that dirty thing in your mouth." The humorist and columnist, Erma Bombeck, wrote a funny column called "Three Little Words." The dictation that follows is excerpted from it.

Dictation ✦ *Write the correct word or number in the blank space. Correct and discuss the dictation.*

_____ _____ _____ _____ _____, we've all raised our kids using a

minimum of three exclamatory sentences: _____! _____! and _____! Used

unsparingly, they can take a parent through _____ or _____ years of living. _____

_____until _____ _____ your homework. No dessert until _____

_____ _____ your plate. No hurry because you're not going. _____ _____.

No_____, _____ movie. No time for your _____? No more_____ _____

_____ _____. No! And _____ the last time I say it.

   Just when you think there are no more ways to say "No," along comes "Don't." Don't _____

_____. Don't forget your _____. Don't _____ _____ _____ _____, do as I say.

Don't _____ to say _____ _____. Don't you hear _____ _____

_____? Don't make me _____it again.

   For sheer drama, there is nothing like "Stop!" Stop _____ . Stop_____

_____ _____. Stop dating _____ _____. Stop acting like

_____a _____ _____. Stop _____to be something you're not.

Stop _____ _____ _____.

   They're all familiar. We _____ _____ _____ without them.

But wouldn't it be _____ if No! Don't! and Stop! were the only things they learned from

us . . . and those three little words shaped their lives.

Discussion ✿   *Discuss these questions with a partner. Share your ideas with the class.*

1._____ What advice do your parents give you now?

2._____ What advice did they give you when you were younger?

3._____ If you're a parent what advice do you give your children?

4._____ Can you think of advice that you've been given, that you didn't take?

5._____ Can you think of who might have said the following, or where you might have seen the following signs?

Don't step on the grass. _____

No smoking on the platform. _____

Don't play your stereo loudly after midnight. _____

No books on your desks during the exam. _____

Don't feed the animals. _____

No drinks served after two A.M. _____

Stop fooling around. _____

No sale without an ID. _____

No children allowed. _____

Now add some of your own:

_____

_____

_____

Sexual Orientation: Questions and Answers

page 133 (CD 1 TRACK 7)

Introduction

Issues surrounding the topic of homosexuality have sparked emotional debate in the nation's capitol and in state legislatures. In this question and answer format, we hope to address some of the misconceptions that may exist. Before you listen, check the meaning of the following sexual orientations :

1. Heterosexuality: a sexual attraction to a person of the opposite sex.
   A heterosexual is often referred to as a straight person.
2. Homosexuality: a sexual attraction to a person of the same sex.
   a. Gay is a synonym for homosexual.
   b. A lesbian is a homosexual woman.
3. Bisexuality: a sexual attraction to both men and women.

Dictation ❀ *Write the correct word or number in the blank space. Correct and discuss the dictation.*

1. *What is sexual orientation?*

   Sexual orientation is an emotional, _____, sexual or affectational attraction to another

   person. It includes heterosexuality, homosexuality, and various forms of _____. Most

   scientists today agree that _____ _____ is most likely the result of a complex

   interaction of_____, cognitive, and environmental factors. In most people, sexual

   orientation is shaped _____ _____ _____ _____.

2. *Is sexual orientation a choice?*

   No. Human beings cannot choose to be either _____ or _____. Mental health

   professionals do not consider sexual orientation to be a _____ _____. There

   is considerable evidence to suggest that biology, including _____ or _____ hormonal

   factors, plays a significant role in a person's sexuality.

3. *Can therapy change sexual orientation?*

   No. Even though most homosexuals live _____, _____ lives, some homosexual

   or bisexual people may seek to change their sexual orientation through therapy because they are

   often _____by family members or religious groups to try and do so. _____ _____

   _____ that homosexuality is not an illness. It does not require treatment and _____ _____

   _____.

4. *Is homosexuality a mental disorder or emotional problem?*

   No. Psychologists and other _____ _____professionals agree that it is not an illness,

   mental_____, or emotional problem. _____ _____is based on 35 years of

   objective, well-designed research.

5. *Why is it important for society to be better educated about homosexuality?*

   _____ _____ _____about sexual orientation and homosexuality is

   likely to diminish _____ – _____ _____. Accurate information is

   especially important to young people who are first discovering and _____ to

   _____their sexuality – whether homosexual, bisexual, or heterosexual.

6. *Is there any legislation against anti-gay violence?*

   Yes. Some states include violence _____ _____ _____ on the basis of

   his or her sexual orientation as a "_____ – _____," and ten U.S. states have laws

   against discrimination _____ _____ _____ _____ sexual orientation.

Discussion ❈ *Discuss these questions with a partner. Share your ideas with the class.*

1. _____ Homosexuals are in every occupation – from doctors, football players, and hair stylists to teachers. Are there certain professions that are more accepting of homosexuals? Some gays are open about their lifestyle and others are "in the closet." Why do some homosexuals prefer to stay in the closet?

2. _____ Many openly gay couples would like to form a legal union of marriage. A civil union for gays is possible only in Vermont. Why do you think gays and lesbians want to be married when they can just live together?

3. _____ There are currently as many as eight million lesbian mothers and gay fathers in the United States. The majority of their children are from previous heterosexual marriages. Why do you think a gay man and woman would marry a heterosexual when these marriages almost always end in divorce?

4. _____ The American Academy of Pediatrics has recently endorsed the right of gay couples to adopt children. Why do you think this organization is now endorsing this kind of adoption?

5. _____ There are countries in the world that still treat homosexuality as a crime or as a disease. Do you know of any countries that do this?

Older Learners *page 135 (CD 1 TRACK 8)*

Introduction

In this unit you will hear about older learners. People are living longer in many countries and a good economy gives older people opportunities that they didn't have earlier. The demographics of universities in the United States are changing. There are many more undergraduate and graduate international students than there were in past decades. There is also another surprising change. What do you think it is?

Pair Dictation ❀ *In the following dictation Student A will read his/ her lines to Student B who has the other half. Student A dictates and Student B writes, then Student B dictates and Student A writes until the paragraph is complete.*

After you decide which student you will be, cover up the other student's dictation.

STUDENT A

Did anyone predict _____ _____ _____ so many adult students? _____

_____ _____ _____ that the number of adults_____ _____

_____ would be so high today. _____ _____ _____

_____ _____ _____ _____, almost half of them are adults _____

_____ _____ _____. The Joe College stereotype – _____ _____ _____

_____ – _____ – _____ full-time student _____ _____ _____

_____ – accounts for only 20 percent _____ _____ _____ _____

_____.

STUDENT B

_____ _____ _____ there would be _____

_____ _____ _____? Nobody in 1980 assumed _____ _____

_____ _____ _____ going to college _____ _____ _____

_____ _____. Of the fifteen million students in college, _____ _____

_____ _____ _____ _____ with kids and jobs. _____ _____

_____ _____ – the 18 to 22-year-old _____ – _____ _____

in residence on campus – _____ _____ _____ _____ _____

of the 15 million students.

Discussion ✿ *Discuss these questions with a partner. Share your ideas with the class.*

1. ____ What are the advantages of having older students in a college class? Are there disadvantages?

2. ____ What are the advantages and disadvantages for the older student?

3. ____ Are you seeing a similar trend in your country?

Dictation ✿ *Write the correct word or number in the blank space. Correct and discuss the dictation.*

This dictation is about an older learner everyone can admire.

For Chi-Hing Wong, _____ _____ _____ _____than _____. That's why at age _____ she decided to go back to school to _____ _____ _____

_____ _____. Next week Wong will don a cap and gown and receive a Boston Public Schools diploma in _____ at Faneuil Hall _____ _____ _____ _____

_____ _____ _____ _____.

"It has always been my dream to go back to school," said Wong , _____ _____ _____

_____ _____ _____ _____ and plans to attend college. "_____ _____

_____ _____ _____ _____, you can learn. It is never too late."

Wong moved to Boston from China in_____. _____ _____ _____ _____ a teacher in China and Okinawa, she did not speak English, _____ _____ _____ _____

_____ _____to teach here. So she went to work in a day care center and concentrated on_____ _____ _____ _____ _____. She also took adult education classes and English classes. When a broken hip forced her to retire _____ _____ _____

_____ _____ _____ _____, Wong saw an opportunity. _____ _____

_____ _____, and she had plenty of free time, but she worried _____ _____ _____

_____ _____ _____ _____ _____ _____ _____.

While visiting her daughter and son-in-law in California, she met a college professor who encouraged her _____ _____ _____ _____. "He could speak _____ languages," Wong recalled. "I told him I wanted to learn, but I was too old. He encouraged me; _____

_____ _____ _____ _____ _____ _____."

Discussion ❀

1. ____ What do you think are some of the problems that Chi-Hing had while getting a high school diploma at the age of 68?

2. ____ Chi-Hing says that she is going on to college. Why would anyone want to get a college degree when they are in their 70s?

3. ____ Chi-Hing was an inspiration to many of the younger students in her class. Have you ever met anyone like her who has inspired you?

Dictation: Judge for Yourself ❀ *Write the correct word or number in the blank space.*

The following is an unusual case about a university student. Before the teacher reads the verdict, decide what the verdict will be.

A man _____ a small university _____ _____ his _____ course of study _____ years earlier. At that time he _____ _____ into student housing and _____ _____ living there ever since. The university tried to _____ the man because he only took an _____ course and never _____ the _____ for a degree. The man _____ he was a student and could not be _____ to leave. The university took the matter to court.

Discussion Before the Verdict ❀

1. ____ Do you think that the court ruled "For" or "Against" the student?
2. ____ Do you know undergraduate or graduate students who are taking a long time or will never finish their degrees? Why are they taking so long?

The Verdict ❀

The court ruled _____ the student and held that it was _____ _____ _____ to decide _____ _____ ___ _____. The man _____ _____ _____ and _____ someone _____ _____ about _____ a _____ _____ the room.

The Psychology of Shopping *page 136 (CD 1 TRACK 9)*

Introduction

We shop for necessities. We also shop for many other reasons. The psychology of shoppers is carefully studied by marketers and the advertising industry. If you're a shopper, you probably already know a lot about the psychology of shopping.

Dictation 1 ❀ *Below are some statements about shopping. After completing the dictation, decide if each of the statements is True or False.*

_____ 1. _____ research _____ found that the color _____ _____ _____ customers feel like spending money.

_____ 2. Upon entering a store, most _____ head _____ ahead.

_____ 3. The only _____ that people shop is that they _____ something.

_____ 4. The _____ reason that people shop on the _____ is that there is no _____ _____.

_____ 5. Women _____ _____ _____ affinity for shopping _____ men.

_____ 6. _____ – _____ surveillance TVs are _____ in stores.

_____ 7. _____ _____ were _____ to reduce shopper _____.

Dictation 2 ❀ *Below are some short excerpts from a book,* **Why We Buy: The Science of Shopping** *by Paco Underhill.*

1. The use of shopping as a _____ _____ seems_____, however. Women like to shop with friends _____ each other on, and _____ each other from ill-advised _____. I don't think _____ see two men _____ _____ on a day of _____ for the _____ bathing suit. As _____ _____, _____ show that when two women shop together, they _____ spend more time and money than women alone. They certainly can _____ and _____ women saddled with _____ companions.

2. Here's an example. The _____ of The Gap and many other clothing stores is that you can easily_____, _____, _____ and otherwise examine at _____ _____ everything on the selling floor. A lot of _____ and _____ are sold thanks to the decision to foster _____ contact between _____ and _____.

Discussion 1 ❀ *Discuss these questions with a partner. Share your ideas with the class.*

1. ____According to Paco Underhill, we use shopping as ___ therapy, ___ reward, ___ bribery, ___ pastime, ___entertainment, ___ an excuse to get out of the house, ___ to kill time. Do you agree? Can you add several more?

2. ____ Is shopping different in your country from shopping in other countries you have been in?

3. ____ Do you sometimes buy things that you hadn't planned on buying? This is called "impulse buying." Tell about one of your "impulse" purchases.

4. ____ Are you very pleased when you buy something "on sale?" Give an example of a great bargain that you got.

5. ____ Have you ever bought anything on the internet? Tell about a good experience or a bad experience you have had with internet shopping. Do you think that internet shopping will eventually become the only way we shop?

Dictation 3 and Decision Making ❀ *Fill in the blanks, make a decision, and discuss it.*

1. You buy a scarf from a discount store as a gift for a friend who is very _____ conscious. You have an empty box from a _____ store. Do you repackage the scarf in the box and give it to your friend?

2. A good friend has _____ _____ a very _____ sweater and _____ you if you like it. You think it is _____. Do you say so?

3. You're in an _____ boutique. While trying on _____ in the _____ _____, you get _____ on a _____ dress. Do you inform the salesperson?

4. You _____ drop your new amplifier and it no longer works. There is no _____ evidence of the accident. Do you try to return it without mentioning the _____?

5. The _____ _____ on the suit you are buying is $280 but the salesperson _____ only _____ _____ $28. Do you ask if there is a _____?

Discussion 2 ❀ *Discuss these questions with a partner. Share your ideas with the class.*

1. ____ Are some of these ethical questions more serious than others? The first two involve lies; three, four, and five involve lies, but also money.

2. ____ In questions three, four, and five, would your answer be different if it was a big store or a little shop owned by one person?

3. ____ Do you think that a person with less money might answer differently from a person for whom money is not a concern?

4. ____ Can you think of any similar situation that you have been in? Tell about it.

Television _page 138 (CD 1 TRACK 10)_

Introduction

Since 1950 when television became a part of people's lives, there have been debates about whether it has enriched our lives, has caused great harm, or done both.

Pair Dictation ❀

Student A will have half of the eight statements and will read his/her lines to Student B, who has the other half. Student A dictates and Student B writes, then Student B dictates and Student A writes until the statements are complete. Then Students A and B together decide whether each statement is "True" or "False."

STUDENT A

____ 1. _____ _____ only 10 % of American homes _____ _____ _____

but by 1990 _____ _____ _____ _____ to 90%.

____ 2. The average American child _____ _____ over 200, 000 acts of violence

on television, _____ _____ _____ before age 18.

____ 3. _____ _____ has been linked _____ _____ _____ _____.

____ 4. Children mostly watch TV _____ _____ _____ _____.

____ 5. _____ _____ _____ _____ have a television. _____ _____,

_____ _____ _____ _____ _____ than a phone.

____ 6. The average child _____ _____ _____ _____ _____ _____

watching television.

____ 7. _____ – ____ _____ _____ _____ _____ _____

identified by a study _____ _____in children's cartoons.

____ 8. Studies show that higher rates of television viewing _____ _____with increased

tobacco usage, _____ _____ _____, and younger onset of

sexual activity.

DO NOT LOOK AT YOUR PARTNER'S PAGE

Pair Dictation ❀

Student A will have half of the eight statements and will read his/her lines to Student B, who has the other half. Student A dictates and Student B writes, then Student B dictates and Student A writes until the statements are complete. Then Students A and B together decide whether each statement is "True" or "False."

STUDENT B

____ 1. In 1980 _____ _____ _____ _____ _____ had a television,

_____ _____ _____ the percentage had grown _____ _____.

____ 2. _____ _____ _____ _____ will witness _____ _____

_____ _____ _____ _____ _____, including 16,000 murders

_____ _____ _____.

____ 3. Watching TV _____ _____ _____ to obesity in children.

____ 4. _____ _____ _____ _____ with friends or family.

____ 5. 95% of homes _____ _____ _____. In fact, more families own a

television _____ _____ _____.

____ 6. _____ _____ _____ spends approximately 56 hours a week

_____ _____.

____ 7. 46% of all television violence _____ _____ _____ _____ took place

_____ _____ _____.

____ 8. _____ _____ _____ _____ _____ _____ _____

_____ are correlated _____ _____ _____

_____, increased alcohol intake, _____ _____ _____

_____ _____ _____.

DO NOT LOOK AT YOUR PARTNER'S PAGE

Dictation 2 ❀ *Write the correct word or number in the blank space. Correct and discuss the dictation.*

Most of us _____ _____ _____ _____ _____ of the addictive
power of television _____ _____ _____ _____ with the medium: _____
_____ _____ _____ _____ _____ too often keeps us _____
_____ _____ _____ _____, from _____ _____ _____,
and from getting involved in community affairs. And yet, _____ _____ _____ _____
_____ _____ _____ _____, or even not turn it on in the first place. _____
_____ _____ _____ _____ _____ ?

Discussion ❀ *Discuss these questions with a partner. Share your ideas with the class.*

1. ____ Do you agree that television can be an addiction?
2. ____ Are you or have you ever been addicted to television?
3. ____ Did your parents regulate how much television you watched?

Dictation 3: Judge for Yourself ❀

The following is an actual case that involved watching too much television. Before the teacher reads the verdict, correct the dictation, and discuss the case.

Jerry, _____ _____ – _____ – _____ _____ _____
_____ _____, broke into his neighbor's house, shot the _____ –
_____ – _____ woman, and escaped in her car. At the trial, _____ _____
_____ _____ _____ to the charges by reason of temporary insanity brought
on by Jerry _____ _____ _____ _____. He watched
_____ _____ _____ _____ _____ _____, _____
_____ _____, and had just watched a movie which contained scenes similar to
_____ _____ _____ _____ _____.

Discussion 2 ❀

1. _____ Do you believe that watching violent scenes on television can lead to violence?
2. _____ How do you think the judge ruled — for or against Jerry?

The Verdict ❀

The court ruled _____ Jerry, stating that there was _____ _____
that _____ _____ the ability to distinguish _____ _____ _____.

Movies *page 139 (CD 1 TRACK 11)*

Introduction

Everyone everywhere enjoys movies. Whether we see a movie in a theater, rent a video to watch at home, or watch a movie on TV, we are transported out of our own lives into other worlds. The following is an advertisement for the movie "My Big Fat Greek Wedding," a very popular romantic comedy.

Dictation ❁ *Write the correct word or number in the blank space. Correct and discuss the dictation.*

Toula is _____. And _____. Which means as a nice Greek girl she's a _____.

All her _____ did the right thing – married Greek boys and made Greek babies.

So everyone _____ – what will _____ _____ Toula?

Then one day she sees the _____ unattainable guy and realizes the only way her life

will get better is if she _____ _____ from her big, fat Greek family. Toula escapes

from the family restaurant. She _____ her seating hostess jacket for a _____

_____, convinces her aunt to give her a new job, and _____ _____ her

coke-bottle glasses for contact lenses, _____ _____ _____ for "him" to walk back

into her life.

Ian Miller is tall, handsome, but definitely not Greek. Their _____ is an Olympian

_____ _____. Can Ian handle Toula, her parents, her aunt, uncles, cousins,

and several _____ of _____ _____? Will Toula discover the love

she's been missing right _____ _____ _____ of her big, fat family?

One thing is _____ _____: for _____ or for _____, for richer or for

_____, with Ian's proposal, Toula is _____ for her big, fat Greek wedding.

Discussion ❀ *Discuss these questions with a partner. Share your ideas with the class.*

1. _____ What is your favorite movie genre? Some people like romantic comedies, but hate action movies. Can you list ten movie genres?

    1. romantic comedies   6. _____

    2. action   7. _____

    3. _____   8. _____

    4. _____   9. _____

    5. _____   10. _____

2. _____ Do you have some favorite movies? What are they?

3. _____ Do you have some favorite actors and actresses? Who are they?

4. _____ Does your country have a movie industry? Are movies exported to other countries?

5. _____ Do you have a rating system like that of the U.S. (G, PG-13, R, etc.)?

6. _____ Would you rather watch a movie in a theater or rent a video and watch it at home? Why?

7. _____ "My Big Fat Greek Wedding" is about a cross-cultural relationship and the concern that parents have about their children marrying outside their own ethnic group. What do you think of this?

Cults on Campus *page 140 (CD 1 TRACK 12)*

Introduction

A cult is an organization. It is frequently religious in nature, and it often follows strange customs and practices. Cults recruit millions of smart people each year and particularly like to prey on college students and people from other countries because people in transition are often looking for groups to join. In this dictation, two college students, Shawn and Karen, share their experiences with a cult recruiter.

Dictation ❀ *Write the correct word or number in the blank space. Correct and discuss the dictation.*

Shawn, student at UCLA:

In the middle of my freshman year, I was having a _____ _____ _____, since I broke up with my girlfriend and my roommate _____ _____ _____ _____ friends. So when this friendly-looking guy came up to me on campus he _____ _____ when I was _____ _____ _____ _____. He was very nice and polite, and we talked about _____ _____ and friends. After a while he asked me to think about coming and _____ _____ _____ he was in where I could make some _____ _____. I decided to _____ _____ _____ _____. But when I was at the second long "meeting" I began to feel I was getting _____ _____ something I wasn't sure about. . . like they started making me _____ _____ _____ _____ about everything I did. Then they made some remarks about how I'd _____ _____ _____ limiting contact with family and friends. Even though I was feeling _____, it didn't feel right. I felt a _____ _____ when I decided not to go back.

Karen, student at NYU:

When I arrived here, I was really excited _____ _____ to a new city to study. It was my first time away from home and I was psyched to _____ _____ _____ my old life and meet new friends. One day in the cafeteria, a _____ – _____ _____, who I thought was a student, _____ _____ and we got talking. At first it was about family and friends, and we really seemed to _____ _____ _____, but later on into the conversation, I _____ _____ that he wasn't a student here. Then he started _____ _____ that I come to his church club where I could make new friends. After a half hour I was getting _____

_____ _____about the way he tried to _____ _____ to me. Finally

I told him to_____ _____. When I wrote about this in my journal to my English professor, she

told me that there are about 3,000 cults _____ _____ the U.S., and that the _____ –

_____ cult, the International Churches of Christ, _____ _____ _____

from at least _____ _____.

Discussion ❀ *Discuss these questions with a partner. Share your ideas with the class.*

1. ____ Do you know of any cults in the U.S. or in your country? What are the purposes of these cults and who are their targets?

2. ____ What techniques do you think cults use to attract people?

3. ____ Why are high-pressure groups so harmful?

4. ____ Some campuses have support groups for victims of cults. What type of person would be vulnerable to joining a cult?

5. ____ How can you tell the difference between a legal religious group and a cult group?

6. ____ Not all cults have religious names or associations. There are other high-pressure groups that can also require total devotion, but instead of a religious agenda, preach revolution, wealth, racism, witchcraft, or superiority. Do you know of any of these groups?

7. ____ What are some reasons why cults continue to survive?

Discussion ❀ *Discuss the following paragraph and questions. Share your ideas with the class.*

A husband and wife who belong to a fundamentalist religious sect based in Attleboro, Massachusetts, were charged with murder of their 10-month-old son who police believe died of starvation. The parents were accused of withholding food and secretly burying their baby in a wooded area. Members of this sect do not believe in traditional medicine or the American legal system. The police became involved to protect present and future children of this particular group. The husband and wife are in their mid-thirties.

Do you think police should step in and prosecute? Why or why not?

Are You Superstitious? *page 141 (CD 1 TRACK 13)*

Introduction

Many educated people will not admit to being superstitious. Their behavior, however, is often different.

Dictation ❀ *Write the correct word or number in the blank space. Correct and discuss the dictation.*

A superstition is an _____ _____ that some action will affect something else _____ _____ _____ _____ _____ _____. Many people believe, _____ _____, that breaking a mirror will result in _____ _____ _____ _____ _____. When one speaks of good fortune, _____ _____ _____ is said to ensure its continuation. _____ _____, rabbits' feet, and other amulets provide insurance to keep the possessor safe.

Many superstitions began _____ _____ _____. The cat has been worshipped by several cultures, including the ancient Egyptian. The fear _____ _____ _____ _____ crossing one's path will bring misfortune may come from the old belief _____ _____ _____.

Many athletes have their own superstitious _____. They often make a connection _____ _____ _____ and some article of clothing, or jewelry. _____ _____ _____ _____, most will reply _____ _____ _____ _____ _____ _____ _____.

Belief in certain superstitions _____ _____ _____ _____ _____. Most people _____ _____ _____ _____ _____ _____ _____ saw their parents doing the same thing _____ _____ _____ _____. They may, _____ _____ _____, know that the original reason was to keep the devil _____ _____ _____ _____.

One danger of superstition is that it encourages people to believe that their future is _____ _____ _____ _____. However, most of us who _____ _____ _____, carry a lucky charm when we fly, and never walk _____ _____ _____ say that our behavior is due to habit or sentiment.

Discussion ❀ *Discuss these questions with a partner. Share your ideas with the class.*

1. _____ Do you believe in some superstitions?

2. _____ Do you practice any superstitions? Why?

3. _____ Here are some common superstitions; are you familiar with any of them?

     a. Placing a bed so that it faces north and south brings misfortune.

     b. If you blow out all the candles on your birthday cake with the first puff, you will get your wish.

     c. If your cheeks suddenly feel on fire, someone is talking about you.

     d. It's bad luck to cut your fingernails at night.

     e. If the palm of your right hand itches, it means you will soon get money.

     f. Never open up an umbrella in your house. It will bring bad luck.

     g. Never have thirteen people around a dinner table because one will die.

     h. If you're moving to a new house, calculate a lucky day for the move or you will have bad luck while you're living there.

4. _____ Share some superstitions from your own culture.

Pair Dictation ❋

In the following dictation you will work in pairs and dictate to each other. Student A will have half of the paragraph and will read her/his lines to Student B, who has the other half. Student A dictates and Student B writes; then Student B dictates and A writes until the paragraph is complete. When you are finished, discuss the paragraph with your partner.

STUDENT A

A young Japanese woman _____ _____ was being wheeled _____ _____ _____ _____ when she noticed the number over the door. _____ _____ _____ _____ softly. _____ _____ _____ _____ and asked what was wrong. _____ _____ _____, but explained that the Japanese character _____ _____ _____ _____ is pronounced the same _____ _____ _____ _____ _____ _____ "_____." Already concerned about her health, _____ _____ _____ to be wheeled _____ _____ _____ _____ "_____." Although she said _____ _____ _____ _____ _____ _____, Keiko was unable _____ _____ _____ _____ _____ _____.

The surgery went well despite the room number, _____ _____ _____ _____ _____ _____. Had the hospital personnel _____ _____ _____ that she was being scheduled _____ _____ _____, her feelings might have become known _____ _____ _____ _____ _____ _____ into a different room. _____ _____ _____, _____ _____, would have been appropriate _____ "_____" _____ _____ _____ also means "life."

Discussion ❋

In the pair dictation, the numbers 3 and 4 both had some significance. Are there numbers in your culture that are either lucky or unlucky? Can you understand how Keiko felt?

Pair Dictation ❀

In the following dictation, you will work in pairs and dictate to each other. Student A will have half of the paragraph and will read his/her lines to Student B, who has the other half. Student A dictates and Student B writes, then Student B dictates and A writes until the paragraph is complete. When you are finished, discuss the paragraph with your partner.

STUDENT B

_____ _____ _____ _____ named Keiko_____ _____

_____ into operating room four _____ _____ _____ _____

_____ _____ _____ _____. She began to cry _____. The nurse

became concerned _____ _____ _____ _____ _____. Keiko

was embarrassed, _____ _____ _____ _____ _____

_____ for the number four _____ _____ _____ _____ as

the character for the word "death." _____ _____ _____ _____

_____, Keiko was disturbed _____ _____ _____ into a room labeled "death."

_____ _____ _____ it was just a silly superstition, _____ _____

_____ to let go of her fear. _____ _____ _____ _____

_____ _____ _____ _____, but the patient suffered needless

anxiety. _____ _____ _____ _____ mentioned to Keiko _____

_____ _____ _____ _____ for room four, _____ _____

_____ _____ _____ _____ in time to reschedule her surgery

_____ _____ _____ _____. Room number three, for example,

_____ _____ _____ _____ because "three" in Japanese characters

_____ _____ "_____."

Discussion ❀

In the pair dictation, the numbers 3 and 4 both had some significance. Are there numbers in your culture that are either lucky or unlucky? Can you understand how Keiko felt?

Make a Difference! Be a Volunteer! *page 142 (CD 1 TRACK 14)*

Introduction

Perry Flicker is one of thousands of volunteers who helped out after the terrorist attacks in New York on September 11, 2001.

Dictation ❀ *Write the correct word or number in the blank space. Correct and discuss the dictation.*

Like millions of other people, Perry Flicker saw the World Trade Center Towers _____

_____ _____. The world's towers, he thought. How could he _____ _____ _____ _____?

So when he heard _____ were needed to deliver water, Gatorade, candy, and _____

to the disaster site, he raced the _____ _____ from his office in New Jersey to what became

known as _____ _____.

After that first _____ and _____ day in ash-covered ruins, he remained there.

For two weeks, Flicker _____ _____ in a personal need to help others, just

as all Americans began a universal, _____ _____ to shore up the _____

_____.

"There were mounds of supplies _____ _____ _____ there, so I couldn't leave," says Flicker,

a _____ production supervisor for Intel Corp. in New Jersey. "I just started working on

the _____. All night, sorting jeans, _____ _____, flashlights, gloves, sweatshirts,

T-shirts. Then it just kept coming. I was up _____ _____ _____ _____

_____ _____ without sleep."

Previously, Flicker was _____ a career volunteer. He had visited sick and lonely senior

citizens. He had helped out with Salvation Army _____. Now, he'll never look at

volunteers, _____ _____ _____.

"I _____ _____ _____ the humility and compassion for people there," he

says. "Firefighters were walking on _____ and _____ metal to try to find

_____, and they were thanking me. Thanking me? _____ _____. Nobody

felt like a hero there. We all just _____ _____ people who had something to do."

Dictation and Discussion ❀

People like Flicker are ordinary citizens who are considered special because they have done something important for society and personify strong character and spirit. Every year one American is chosen to receive The USA Award; you and your classmates will choose the winner from the six finalists below.

Fill in the blank spaces with the word or words you hear. Then discuss each candidate for the award with a partner. After you have chosen your winner together, share your decision with the class. The class then discusses the options and votes to elect one finalist.

_____ 1. Josh Ryan, 48, of Bandera, Texas, invested $10,000,000 from his _____ _____

   _____ to open Ryan Ranch, a home to _____ young adults, many of

   whom have been _____ _____ _____.

_____ 2. Leon Goldberg, 68, of Detroit, Michigan, kept his _____ workers on the _____

   after a fire destroyed his _____ _____ last year. He _____ the plant, and all

   but _____ are now _____ _____ _____ _____.

_____ 3. LaToya Jefferson, 51, of Milltown, Florida, is a _____ at Paula's Place, a _____

   _____ for African-American women. She has been there to cook for _____ hours

   a day for _____ years and remains _____ with the women, _____ _____

   _____ _____.

_____ 4. Addie May Carlson, 75, of Oakdale, California, _____ _____ _____ low-

   cost summer camps for disabled children for five years. She accepts _____ _____.

_____ 5. Bob Dean, 36, of Chicago, Illinois, grew up in a poor _____ and knows what it's like

   to be on _____. One day he _____ _____ at the courthouse and

   offered to help kids in _____. He's been volunteering for _____ years, sometimes

   _____ _____ a week. "I've seen _____ _____ _____ _____," he says.

_____ 6. Lena Chin, 52 , of New York City, arrived from China in _____ and soon began

   _____ several days a week in her city's Chinatown to help Asian _____

   whose _____ to speak or read English makes it impossible for them to fill

   out the _____ forms required for _____ _____.

Winning in Las Vegas *page 144 (CD 1 TRACK 15)*

Introduction

Have you ever won money in a lottery or card game, or at a gambling casino? Many people go to Las Vegas with the dream of winning "big bucks." Here is a letter to the advice columnist, Ann Landers, from a woman who really did win, but then her problems began!

Dictation ❈ *Write the correct word or number in the blank space. Correct and discuss the dictation.*

I need an unbiased person with a good _____ _____ _____ to help me sort this out. A woman I work with (_____ _____ friends) decided we should take our vacation together and go to Las Vegas and _____, just _____ _____ _____ _____ _____. Nellie and I saved all year, and each of us was able to _____ $_____ for the trip. After travel and hotel expenses, we had just $_____ _____ for gambling.

Nellie and I _____ ____ _____ _____, saw some great shows, and _____ _____ _____. We lost some money at blackjack and the craps tables so we stopped and went for the _____ _____, which we both love. We each had $_____ left, and decided to play the _____ _____ machines.

By 2:30 A.M., we were _____ _____, and all the money we had _____ _____ for gambling was gone. Nellie started to walk back to our rooms. I then said, "I'm going to put one last dollar in and _____ _____ _____." I stepped over to the slot that Nellie _____ _____ _____ all night, put in a dollar, and lo and behold, I _____ _____ _____! The money was _____ all over the floor, and it seemed like an _____ _____ of silver dollars was coming out. I _____ _____ _____, and it came to $1,200.

Nellie _____, "You have to _____ _____ _____ _____. I fed that machine all night!" I replied, "When you _____ _____, it became my machine. I _____ _____ _____ anything." She yelled, "What kind of a friend are you, _____?" Well, I realized our friendship was _____ _____, and decided to _____ _____ _____ with Nellie.

I would like to know, _____ _____ _____ _____ to do it, or was I _____ _____ to share my winnings? Please tell me what you think. Tess in Texas.

Discussion 1 ❀ *Discuss these questions with a partner. Share your ideas with the class.*

Work with a partner or small group and think of a response to this woman.

Discussion 2 ❀

1. _____ With a small group tell what you know about these different forms of gambling.

        Casino gambling   Sports betting
        Dog races   Horse races
        State lotteries   Card games

2. _____ What about in your country? Is gambling legal? Give reasons why it is not legal in some countries.

3. _____ In the United States there is an organization called "Gamblers Anonymous" that helps people who are addicted to gambling. What kind of help would you expect this organization to give?

4. _____ In the United States, many Native Americans are allowed to build casinos on their own land (reservations) and are not subject to state lottery laws. One example of this is in Connecticut where two reservations, Foxwoods and Mohegan Sun, have been very popular and are expanding every year. Should Native Americans be allowed to do this? Why or why not?

A Business That's "Going to the Dogs"

page 145 (CD 1 TRACK 16)

Introduction

Americans love their pets and treat them like members of the family. Recent statistics show that Americans have more than 500 million pets. It's not surprising, therefore, to learn that pet-related businesses are popping up everywhere.

Americans are not alone in their love of animals. People in many countries of the world form strong emotional bonds with their pets. Pet worship is not a new cultural norm, either. Ancient Egyptians shaved off their eyebrows to mourn their pet cats that died.

Discussion ❀ *Talk about the photograph and read the caption under it. These dogs get picked up every morning and dropped off every night. Where do you think these dogs are going?*

With their seat belts secure, these passengers are set for the ride to the Common Dog, where they spend their days.

Dictation ❀ *Write the correct word or number in the blank space. Correct and discuss the dictation.*

The following interview is between dog day care owner and manager Richard Ross and a reporter.

Reporter: Richard, how did you get into the _____ _____ _____ business?

Richard: It all started when I agreed to _____ _____ _____ a neighbor's dog when she

went on vacation for a week. She didn't want to put her dog _____ _____ _____

and since I have two dogs _____ _____ _____, I said sure. Then when a

friend had to take a _____ _____ to Texas, he asked me to pet-sit his dogs.

Then _____ _____ _____ and more and more working people who

worried about their dogs getting lonely during the day started calling me up. _____

_____ _____ _____ _____ and here I am!

Reporter: So how many dogs do you have in your dog day care business now?

Richard: _____ _____; some days we have ten dogs, but we're licensed for _____.

Reporter: Do all of the dogs come for day care while their owners are_____ _____?

Richard: No, some come for _____ _____ _____ _____ _____ _____ _____ while

the owners are on vacation. We have _____ _____ and _____ _____.

Reporter: _____ _____! What _____ _____ _____ do you charge?

Richard: If the owner _____ _____ his dog, we charge $28.00 a day. If they want _____

– _____ _____ _____ in our van, the charge is higher, about 35 _____.

Reporter: You provide transportation?

Richard: Yup. _____ pick up the dogs beginning at 7:30 AM from their homes and drop them

off at 5:00 PM. Dogs love _____ _____!

Reporter: Do you have any special _____ _____?

Richard: Well, they have to be _____, of course. And they must have written proof

of rabies and _____ _____. Once in a while there's a dog that doesn't

_____ _____ _____ other dogs, but most love being here with

their _____.

Reporter: I can see that you love your job.

Richard: You've _____ _____ _____ to do this. And now that business

_____ _____, I can hire more help!

Discussion ❀ *Discuss these questions with a partner. Share your ideas with the class.*

Here is a questionnaire asked of thousands of Americans. Guess what percent of Americans pay special attention to their cats and dogs. Your teacher will give you the answers. What information surprised you?

Example: 49% of dog owners prepare and cook special food for them.

_____ give their pets Christmas or birthday presents

_____ cook special food for their cats

_____ talk to their pets on the phone or answering machine

_____ call themselves the animal's mother or father

_____ sometimes dress up their pets for special occasions, such as Halloween

_____ sign letters or cards from themselves and their pets

_____ send their dogs to dog day care

Discussion ❀

1. _____ What pets are popular in your country?

2. _____ In your country do:

> dogs live inside or outside the home?
> pets ever sleep with people?
> people cook special food for their pets?
> people have unusual pets such as monkeys, pigs, or crickets?
> people have animal hospitals and animal cemeteries?
> people have dog day care businesses?

3. _____ Studies show that people's blood pressure drops when they talk to their pets. Think of some other advantages of having pets.

> -for children
> -for the elderly
> -for the handicapped

Animal Idioms ❀

In the title of this unit, the expression "going to the dogs" is an idiom. Usually this expression means "deteriorating." Here are some other animal idioms and expressions for you to discuss with your teacher.

1. She works like a dog.
2. He puts on the dog.
3. Let sleeping dogs lie.
4. He leads a dog's life.
5. They asked for a doggie bag at the restaurant.
6. We're in the dog days of summer.
7. She let the cat out of the bag.
8. I sent the letter by snail mail.

Careers *page 146 (CD 1 TRACK 17)*

Introduction

Most people want to work at a job they enjoy. They would like to look forward to doing this job every day, possibly for forty years. Sometimes they don't prepare for such a career because the salary and status of the job are not high.

Dictation ❀ *Below are average annual salaries for various jobs. These are average and approximate. Fill the blank spaces with the salaries you hear.*

1. computer engineer _____

2. librarian _____

3. public school teacher _____

4. accountant _____

5. lawyer _____

6. web designer _____

7. preschool teacher _____

8. university professor _____

9. doctor _____

10. manager and senior executive _____

_____

and here are some exceptional ones:

11. Vice-President of the U.S. _____

12. 30-year-old female singer _____
    (like Madonna)

13. professional athlete _____
    (football quarterback)

14. 43-year-old male comedian _____
    (like Seinfeld)

Discussion ❀ *Discuss these questions with a partner. Share your ideas with the class.*

1. _____ Did any of these salaries surprise you? Are they similar to salaries in your country?

2. _____ Does the person who has the most education make the most money?

3. _____ Is salary very important to you when choosing a career?

Dictation ❀ *Write the correct word or number in the blank space. Correct and discuss the dictation.*

This is an excerpt from the book *Palace of Desire* by the Egyptian novelist Naguib Mafouz.

The father_____ his hand _____. He_____ to want to tell his son, "You must exercise a little patience and not leap to a decision on something you know nothing about." Then he_____, "It's just as I said. For that reason _____ _____ attracts students from good families. And there's the teaching profession. Do you know anything about teaching or is your information limited to the Teacher's College? It's a miserable profession _____ _____ _____ _____ _____ _____. I'm well _____about what's said of such matters, but you're young and inexperienced. _____ _____ _____ _____ _____ _____ _____ _____ _____. It's an occupation uniting people who have modern educations with the products of traditional religious education. It's one utterly devoid of grandeur and esteem. I'm _____ _____ men of distinction and civil servants who have _____ _____ to allow their daughters to marry a teacher, _____ _____ _____ _____ _____ _____."

The son was sorry but could only repeat with all the politeness and delicacy he could muster, a phrase he had_____ _____ in his reading. "_____ _____ _____ _____ _____ _____."

The father, Al-Said Ahmad, _____ _____ _____ _____ between Kamal and the wardrobe, as though appealing to an invisible person for confirmation of the absurdity of the idea _____ _____ _____ _____. Then he said indignantly, "Really? _____ _____ _____ _____ _____ to hear drivel like this? You imply there's a difference _____ _____ _____ _____. There's no true knowledge _____ _____ _____ _____."

Discussion ❀ *Discuss these questions with a partner. Share your ideas with the class.*

1. _____ Do you agree with the son's final statement? With the father's final statement?
2. _____ Have your parents or other older relatives ever said to you what Kamal's father said to him?

Taxes! Taxes! Taxes! *page 147 (CD 1 TRACK 18)*

Introduction

How much do you know about the different types of taxes that Americans pay?
Take this quick true/false/maybe quiz. Discuss this with your class.

___ 1. All Americans who work, even part-time, pay income taxes.
___ 2. All Americans pay a federal income tax.
___ 3. All Americans pay a state income tax.
___ 4. All Americans pay a city income tax.
___ 5. All Americans pay a state sales tax.
___ 6. All Americans pay a property tax.
___ 7. All Americans who work pay a social security tax.
___ 8. Some Americans have to pay a fuel tax, a cigarette tax, and an inheritance tax.

Dictation ❀ *Write the correct word or number in the blank space. Correct and discuss the dictation.*

Americans say that there are only two guarantees in life: _____ and taxes. Of all the rituals of

American life, none is more certain than _____ _____ yearly tax forms. Compare the

_____ _____ of these two single women.

(The figures below do not include deductions for insurance or retirement plans.)

	Maria Collins	Suzanne Davis
Income/weekly	$400.00	$1,500.00
Federal Income Tax	_____	_____
State Income Tax	_____	_____
Social Security Tax	_____	_____
Take-home pay	_____	_____

State and Local Taxes

Every state acquires the necessary _____ to maintain its government through tax collection,

fees, and licenses. The Federal Government also _____ money to the 50 states. With the revenue

that the states receive from the Federal Government, taxes, licenses, and fees, they provide _____

_____ to their citizens. Examples of these services are public schools, police _____,

health and _____ benefits, and the operation of the state government.

Among the _____ _____ _____ _____ that many states impose are personal

_____ tax, corporate income tax, _____ _____, and real _____ tax.

Personal Income Tax

Most states _____ their residents to pay a personal income tax. These states generally use one or two _____ __ _____ income tax. These two methods are the _____ income tax and the _____ _____ income tax, and both methods require the taxpayer to figure his or her _____ _____. Massachusetts residents, for example, pay a flat rate of _____ for the state income tax, but all Americans pay a graduated _____ income tax. Pity the "_____" New Yorker who lives and works in New York City. This person has to pay _____ income taxes: federal, state, and _____ _____!

State Sales Taxes

A sales tax is _____ on the sale of goods and services. Very often you pay sales tax when you buy something. The consumer tax system taxes the _____ _____. The _____ at a store collects the tax from the buyer and then sends the _____ _____ to the state. The percent of the sales taxes _____ from state to state. For example, in Massachusetts, it's _____ and in Hawaii, it's _____. So if you bought a car in Massachusetts for $20,000, you'd pay ___ _____ ____ _____.

What states decide to tax _____ as well. In some states there is a tax on food, clothing, _____, newspapers, and utilities. In addition, certain groups are often _____ from paying sales tax. Religious, educational, and charitable groups are _____ _____ from paying sales tax under certain circumstances. A large _____ of a state's sales tax revenue goes toward _____, public welfare, and the running of state government. _____ _____ this, many states consider the sales tax to be the most important tax _____ _____.

There are a few states that have no sales tax. One such state is _____ _____. But _____ _____ (on houses, factories, and boats) there are _____ _____.

Discussion ❀ *Discuss these questions with a partner. Share your ideas with the class.*

1. ____ In the above article, a graduated income tax and a flat-rate income tax are mentioned. A graduated tax is based on the idea that the more money you make, the more taxes you pay. Which tax is more equitable, the graduated or the flat rate? Why?

2. _____ If you lived and worked in Massachusetts and decided to buy a car in New Hampshire, where there is no sales tax, you would still have to pay the sales tax. Why?

3. _____ If you lived in Massachusetts but worked in New Hampshire, where there is no state income tax, you would still have to pay a state income tax. Why?

4. _____ If most people in Massachusetts want to change the state income tax from a flat rate to a graduated tax, can they do it? How?

5. _____ Can you name some countries where there are no taxes? Where does the government get the revenue to pay for public services?

6. _____ Compare the income tax system in your country to that in the United States.

7. _____ Compute the annual salaries of Maria Collins and Suzanne Davis. What kind of job do you think these women have?

The Trials of Tipping *page 149 (CD 1 TRACK 19)*

Introduction

Many international students and tourists are confused about the system of tipping when they come to the United States. The rules for tipping are very illogical and even Americans aren't always sure what kind of tip to leave. Let's say that your waitress was great, but your taxi driver was scary and your hair stylist was terrible. What do you do? Here is some help in figuring out the tipping dilemma.

Dictation ❀ *Write the correct word or number in the blank space. Correct and discuss the dictation.*

Tipping says "_____ _____" for good service, explains Judy Bowman, president of Protocol Consultants International, who _____ _____ training businesses and corporations in business and _____ _____. According to Bowman, the _____ _____ _____ for tipping has gone up in the last year, from _____ percent to _____ percent. "If you leave a 10 or 15% tip, you're going to get _____ _____."

The most important thing to remember about tipping is that you tip members of the _____ _____ — people who rely on tips to make a living, _____ _____ _____. Think about your waiter as the guy who sits next to you in economics class and your _____ _____ may change. Major tipping situations that people _____ _____ on a regular basis include trips to the _____ _____, restaurants, taxis, _____, and food delivery services. For each service, a basic tip is required, but it's_____ _____ _____ to decide how much to give. For someone who goes _____ and _____ the call of duty, you would give a tip closer to the 20% range. For example, when ordering pizza, use the time as a _____ _____ _____. If you're told the pizza will arrive in 20 minutes, but it comes in 15, you _____ _____ _____. On the other hand, if the pizza is late or you've had a _____ _____ dealing with people in the _____ office, you are _____ _____ to tip _____ or not at all. If you are not going to tip, _____ _____. This way the delivery guy will know what he's done wrong. The same _____ _____ _____ should follow with taxi drivers, hairstylists, and waiters. But if you often go to the same hairstylist or restaurant and the service is good, tip well. The _____ _____ _____ _____!

Discussion ❀ *Discuss these questions with a partner. Share your ideas with the class.*

1. _____ In the article above, the consultant recommends that if the service is bad, you should leave no tip. Another consultant may disagree with her. Why? What about taxi drivers and hair-stylists – what would YOU do?

2. _____ Would you complain if you think the service is bad? If so, would you complain to the server or to the management?

3. _____ What are you looking for in service: informal friendliness? efficiency? formal correctness?

4. _____ Have you ever seen "tip cups" in coffee shops and ice cream parlors asking for small change? You don't have to leave a tip. Can you explain why?

5. _____ If you don't know whether or not to tip someone, what's the best thing to do?

6. _____ According to the above article, Bowman says the tipping rate has gone up in the last year. Can you imagine a situation when the going rate might go down?

7. _____ Can you explain why a waiter in a high class restaurant makes more on tips than a waiter in a low class restaurant – even though they both work equally hard?

Discussion ❀ *Discuss these questions with a partner. Share your ideas with the class.*

1. What is the tipping custom in your country? Is tipping a good system?

2. From the list, guess and check ( ) the people Americans don't tip:

___ pizza delivery person   ___ flower delivery person
___ mail delivery person   ___ massage person
___ package delivery person   ___ bartender
___ newspaper delivery person   ___ hotel porter
___ security guard   ___ housepainter
___ gas station attendant   ___ mechanic
___ airport luggage porter   ___ manicurist

Hold the Pickles, Hold the Lettuce

page 150 (CD 1 TRACK 20)

Introduction

The McDonald's Corporation has become a powerful symbol of America's service economy, the sector now responsible for ninety percent of the country's new jobs. In 1968, McDonald's operated about 1,000 restaurants. By the year 2000 it had about 23,000 restaurants worldwide and opens roughly 2,000 new ones each year.

Prediction Dictation ❀

In this dictation you are __not__ going to listen first. Work with a partner and fill in each blank with a word you think is correct. When you are finished, you will listen and do the dictation on the next page. Then compare your responses.

What is perhaps _____ astonishing about America's fast _____ business is just how successful it _____ become: what began in the 1940s as a handful of hot dog and hamburger stands in Southern California _____ spread like kudzu across the land to become a $110 billion industry. _____ _____ Eric Schlosser, the author of *Fast Food Nation*, _____ now spend more on _____ _____ _____ they spend on higher _____, personal computers, _____ software, or new cars, or on movies, books, videos, and recorded music combined. Mr. Schlosser writes that on any given day in the _____ _____ about one quarter of the adult population visits a fast food _____, and that the typical _____ now consumes approximately three hamburgers and four orders of French _____ every week.

"An estimated one of _____ eight workers in the United States has at some time been employed _____ McDonald's," he adds, and the company hires more _____ than any other American organization, public or _____.

As fast _____ franchises from McDonald's to Pizza _____ to Kentucky Fried _____ go global, this dynamic has assumed international flavor. In Brazil, Mr. Schlosser reports, McDonald's _____ _____ the nation's largest private employer. _____ at McDonald's Hamburger University in Oak Park, Illinois, are now taught in 20 different _____, and a Chinese anthropologist notes that all the _____ in a primary school in Beijing recognized an image of Ronald McDonald. For the _____, the anthropologist noted, McDonald's represents "Americana and the promise of modernization."

Listening Dictation ❀ *Write the correct word in the blank space. Correct and discuss the dictation.*

What is perhaps _____ astonishing about America's fast _____ business is just how successful it _____ become: what began in the 1940s as a handful of hot dog and hamburger stands in Southern California _____ spread like kudzu across the land to become a $110 billion industry. _____ _____ Eric Schlosser, the author of *Fast Food Nation,* _____ now spend more on _____ _____ _____ they spend on higher _____, personal computers, _____ software, or new cars, or on movies, books, videos, and recorded music combined. Mr. Schlosser writes that on any given day in the _____ _____ about one quarter of the adult population visits a fast food _____, and that the typical _____ now consumes approximately three hamburgers and four orders of French _____ every week.

"An estimated one of _____ eight workers in the United States has at some time been employed _____ McDonald's," he adds, and the company hires more _____ than any other American organization, public or _____.

As fast _____ franchises from McDonald's to Pizza _____ to Kentucky Fried _____ go global, this dynamic has assumed international flavor. In Brazil, Mr. Schlosser reports, McDonald's _____ _____ the nation's largest private employer. _____ at McDonald's Hamburger University in Oak Park, Illinois are now taught in twenty different _____, and a Chinese anthropologist notes that all the _____ in a primary school in Beijing recognized an image of Ronald McDonald. For the _____, the anthropologist noted, McDonald's represents "Americana and the promise of modernization."

Discussion ❦ *Discuss these questions with a partner. Share your ideas with the class.*

1. ____ Why do you think fast food restaurants are so popular? Can you list five reasons?

2. ____ What do critics of fast food restaurants say about them? Can you list five criticisms?

3. ____ Do you have American fast food restaurants in your country? Do they have different items on the menu because they are in a different country? Do you have fast food restaurants that are specific to your country?

4. ____ Which is your favorite fast food restaurant and what is your favorite meal?

Restaurant Vocabulary

Work with a partner and see if you know the meaning of the following. Do you know any other idiomatic food expressions that you can add to this list?

1. Hold the pickle, hold the lettuce.

2. I want that "to go."

3. Go easy on the salt.

4. Light on the dressing.

5. I'll have it medium rare.

6. I want my eggs sunny side up.

7. I'll have my eggs over easy.

8. I'll have my coffee black.

9. Heavy on the pickles, please.

10. I'll have a breast and a leg.

11. I'd like my dressing on the side.

12. Give me the works.

The People's Court *page 151 (CD 1 TRACK 21)*

Introduction

People's Courts are also known as Small Claims Courts. These courts are open to anyone who has a disagreement about an amount of money between $500 and $5000. A person does not need a lawyer. A judge listens to the case and makes a common sense decision. In this unit you will hear four typical cases that come before these courts.

Dictation ❀ *Fill in the blanks and then with a partner, decide who should pay whom and how much.*

CASE 1. Two women gave their _____ an $800 _____ _____ before moving into their apartment. When they moved out three years later, the landlord _____ to return the $800. He said that the women had left _____ in the walls from _____ pictures and _____ on the carpet. The women claimed the slight damage was from normal _____ and _____ of apartment living. In court the landlord produced _____ totaling $1500 for painting and cleaning he had done.

CASE 2. Your local _____ _____ lost your winter coat, _____ at $500, but refused to pay the full _____ because they say it's only _____ $200.

CASE 3. The auto shop repaired something you didn't _____, _____ you for it, and refused to _____ the car until you paid for it with a _____ check or cash. You _____, but needed your car, so you paid. You demand the _____ back.

CASE 4. The 12-year-old kid next door hit a baseball _____ your window. His parents say it's his responsibility to pay for it. But his weekly _____ is $4.00, and it would take three years to _____ the _____ _____.

Discussion ❀ *Discuss these questions with a partner. Share your ideas with the class.*

1. ____ What would you do if you lent a friend $300 but he/she only paid you back $100?
2. ____ You returned a defective piece of $600 luggage to the store, but the store refuses to give you a refund. What do you do?
3. ____ Your ex-fiancee won't return the $2000 diamond engagement ring you gave her. You called off the engagement three months ago. What do you do?

Retirement $\quad$ _page 151 (CD 1 TRACK 22)_

Introduction

Many people dream about retirement. They think about not having to get up early in the morning to commute to work five days a week. They think about golf and travel and having the time to do whatever they want to do. But the reality is sometimes different.

Prediction Dictation ❀

In this dictation you are <u>not</u> going to listen first. Work with a partner and fill in each blank with a word you think is correct. When you are finished, you will listen to the same article and do the dictation on the next page. Then compare your responses.

Jane: And now to our roving reporter, Roger, _____ _____ bring you a second report on

retirement issues.

Roger: Thank you, Jane. In the _____ report on Tuesday night I mentioned that _____

_____ 2.6 million people _____ _____ _____ of 65 working full-_____

and 2.9 working _____-time. I am here at Adams' Supermarket, one of a six-state chain

of supermarkets in the Northeast, and with me is Bob, an employee who has agreed _____

_____ interviewed. Hello, Bob.

Bob: _____, _____.

Roger: Can I ask you _____ _____ _____ _____?

Bob: I'm 73, and I've been working here in the produce department for six _____. You can

see me here 30 _____ _____ _____.

Roger: Is this what you've _____ done?

Bob: No, I drove a _____ for the Tropical Banana Company for 32 years, and now I'm

stocking _____ at Adams' Supermarket. I can't get away from _____.

Roger: So what made you do this?

Bob: I'll tell you, Roger. I _____ _____ 65 and for two years I did _____.

My wife said I was driving her _____. One _____ I came in here to buy some

milk and I saw someone who looked much _____ than me bagging groceries.

I applied for a job and I've been here ever _____.

Roger: So when do you think you'll give it up?

Bob: Probably when I'm _____ or if I die – whichever comes first. I like feeling that I can still do things and do them well, and now my wife is happy to see me when I come_____.

Roger: Thank you _____ _____, Bob, for speaking with us. The manager of the store _____ told _____ that the Adams' stores have 276 _____ over 70, 29 _____ 80, and two over _____, so Bob might get his wish. He also said that he wished he had many more older _____. He appreciates their life experience and their sense of _____. I'll be back next Tuesday to talk _____those workers over 65 for whom retirement is just a dream _____ their nest eggs are falling short.

Listening Dictation ✿ *Write the correct word in the blank space. Correct and discuss the dictation.*

Dave: And now to our roving reporter, Roger, _____ _____bring you a second report on retirement issues.

Roger: Thank you, Dave. In the _____ report on Tuesday night I mentioned that _____ _____ 2.6 million people _____ _____ _____ of 65 working full-_____ and 2.9 working _____ -time. I am here at Adams' Supermarket, one of a six-state chain of supermarkets in the Northeast, and with me is Bob, an employee who has agreed _____ _____ interviewed. Hello, Bob.

Bob: _____, _____.

Roger: Can I ask you _____ _____ _____ _____?

Bob: I'm 73, and I've been working here in the produce department for six _____. You

can see me here 30 _____ ____ _____.

Roger: Is this what you've _____ done?

Bob: No, I drove a _____ for the Tropical Banana Company for 32 years and now I'm

stocking _____ at Adams' Supermarket. I can't get away from _____.

Roger: So what made you do this?

Bob: I'll tell you, Roger. I _____ _____ 65 and for two years I did _____. My

wife said I was driving her _____. One _____ I came in here to buy some milk and

I saw someone who looked much _____ than me bagging groceries. I applied for

a job and I've been here ever _____.

Roger: So when do you think you'll give it up?

Bob: Probably when I'm _____ or if I die – whichever comes first. I like feeling that I can still

do things and do them well, and now my wife is happy to see me when I come _____.

Roger: Thank you _____ _____, Bob, for speaking with us. The manager of the store _____

told _____ that the Adams' stores have 276 _____ over 70, 29 _____ 80, and

two over _____, so Bob might get his wish. The manager also said that he wished

he had many more older _____. He appreciates their life experience and their

sense of _____. I'll be back next Tuesday to talk _____ those workers over

65 for whom retirement is just a dream _____ their nest eggs are falling short.

Discussion ❀ *Discuss these questions with a partner. Share your ideas with the class.*

1. ____ Many of the people who work at the cash registers, stock the shelves, and bag groceries in
our supermarkets are senior citizens, immigrants, or teenagers. What are some of the reasons
for this?

2. ____ When do people in your country retire? Do women retire before men?

Childhood *page 153 (CD 1 TRACK 23)*

Introduction

Humans have the longest childhood. In developed countries, we can say that childhood lasts for approximately eighteen years and for many people it is a happy time of endless play, free from many responsibilities.

Discussion ❀ *Decide whether you agree or disagree with the statement.*

_____1. Childhood is a time for learning, not working.

_____2. It is good for teenagers to have part-time jobs.

_____3. Children should not expect to earn money for doing work in their own homes.

_____4. Children should receive a weekly allowance to be spent freely.

Dictation ❀ *Write the correct word in the blank space. Correct and discuss the dictation.*

_____ – _____ – _____Tracy has a _____, _____, and _____ in her room. Her parents buy her the latest CDs, and they give her a _____ _____ _____ _____.

"If I want something, or I need something, I just say, '_____ _____ _____ _____ _____?' says the South Boston eighth-grader. "_____ _____ _____ _____ _____ _____ _____ _____ _____, my parents give me money. They don't tell me no, really."

Tracy, _____, says _____ _____ _____. She does not have a cell phone, _____ _____, unlike many of her friends.

She is the new face _____ _____ _____ _____, a member of a generation that has _____ _____ during an era of almost _____ _____.

Nearly a _____ ____ _____ _____ _____ _____ _____.

They eat out _____ _____ _____ at least _____ _____ _____.

The average American teen spent more than _____ a week in _____, _____ _____ the marketing research firm Teenage Research Unlimited — _____ _____ _____ just four years earlier. About _____ – _____ of that is money they can spend_____ _____ _____;

the rest is for specific items such as groceries.

That makes teenagers a marketer's dream. But analysts say their spending _____ — developed

during _____ _____ _____ _____ _____ — will probably make them _____

_____. Some worry that the intense adolescent focus on consuming will _____ _____

a future in which an even greater number of Americans are living _____ _____ _____.

Discussion ❀ *Discuss these questions with a partner. Share your ideas with the class.*

1. _____ Is the preceding information surprising to you? Why or why not?
2. _____ Do you see any similar trends in your country?
3. _____ Does it make any difference if the teenager who spends over a hundred dollars a
week has a part-time job and is earning this spending money?
4. _____ Were there things you wanted as a teenager that your parents would not buy for
you because they were concerned about "spoiling you?"

Dictation ❀ *Write the correct word or number in the blank space. Correct and discuss the dictation.*

In contrast, there are many children in the world who are engaged in extreme and hazardous forms of work, and who are being robbed of their fundamental right to a childhood.

_____ _____ _____ that about _____ million children between the ages of _____ _____ _____ work at least full-time. If children for whom work is a _____ _____ are _____, the figure reaches _____ _____. Sixty-one percent of these were in _____, _____ in Africa, and _____ in Latin America. Most working children in_____ _____ were found in _____; _____ children worked in _____ and services, with fewer in _____, _____, and _____ _____.

Conditions of child labor range from that of four-year-olds _____ to rug looms to keep them from running away, to seventeen-year-olds _____ _____ on the family farm. In some cases, a child's work can be _____ to him or her and to the family; _____ _____ _____ can be a positive experience in a child's _____ _____. This depends largely on the age of the child, the conditions in which the child works, and whether work _____ _____ _____ _____ _____ _____ _____. In addition, more than_____ children, some _____ _____ _____ _____, are child soldiers and are_____ _____ in _____ different _____ around the world.

Discussion ❀ *Discuss these questions with a partner. Share your ideas with the class.*

1. ____ Is this information surprising to you? Why or why not?
2. ____ Are there many children who are working and not going to school in your country?
3. ____ Are there any children who are soldiers in your country?
4. ____ Is there anything that individuals can do about these situations?
5. ____ Should we ban imports of products made by children?

Chinese New Year *page 155 (CD 1 TRACK 24)*

Introduction

New Year's Eve and New Year's Day are major holidays in all cultures because there is a universal hope that one can begin anew. Because of different lunar and solar calendars, the holidays are celebrated at different times of the year and in different ways. The one thing that is not different is that there are special symbolic foods for the New Year whenever it is celebrated. Americans toast the New Year with champagne. Jews dip apples or bread in honey hoping for a sweet year. The Chinese, too, have many symbolic foods.

Dictation ❀ *Write the correct word or number in the blank space. Correct and discuss the dictation.*

In feudal times, the Chinese believed that the eve of the New Year marked the Kitchen God's

departure to heaven _____ _____ _____ _____ _____ _____

_____. To welcome the Kitchen God _____ _____ _____ _____

in the New Year, each family feasted and performed a "spring-cleaning." The spring festival symbolized

_____ _____ _____ and the earth's seasonal return to life.

"We serve _____ _____ that are auspicious for the New Year," Danny Woo, the

manager at the Jumbo Seafood Restaurant in _____, says. He is planning an _____

_ _____ _____ _____, because eight in Chinese _____ _____ _____

_____, since it sounds like the word "_____."

_____ _____ are made only in their whole form to represent a year

_____ _____ _____ _____ _____.

One traditional Chinese _____ for the New Year is Clams in Black Bean _____,

because their _____ resemble Chinese coins, which _____ _____.

Another _____ recipe is Good Luck Dumplings.

Pair Dictation ❀

Student A will have half of the recipe for Good Luck Dumplings, and will read his/her part to Student B, who has the other half. Student A dictates and Student B writes, then Student B dictates and A writes.

STUDENT A

Good Luck Dumplings

Ingredients

1 lb. (pound) pork, beef, or tofu, drained of excess liquid

____ _____ ____ _____

1 clove minced garlic

_____ _____ _____ _____ _____ _____

1/4 teaspoon pepper

_____ _____ _____ _____

1 cup chopped green onions

____ _____ _____ _____ _____ _____

Vegetables of your choice

Directions

1. In a large bowl, combine all dumpling ingredients* except wonton wrappers, and mix thoroughly.
2. Wrap about 1 1/2 tablespoons of filling in wonton wrappers. With finger tips, lightly wet edges of wrappers with water. Firmly pinch edges. Repeat until all filling has been used.
3. Place dumplings in slightly salted boiling water, and cook gently for about 10 minutes. Drain; then run cold water over cooked dumplings to avoid sticking.
*If adding vegetables, make sure to blanch them and drain them of excess liquid before combining.

For Soup:
   1 pot of chicken broth, boiling
   Chopped green onions as desired for garnish

1. Add dumplings to boiling chicken broth and cook until done.
2. Garnish with green onions and serve.

Discussion ❀ *Discuss these questions with a partner. Share your ideas with the class.*

1. ____ What special or symbolic foods does your family prepare for your New Year or any other important holiday?
2. ____ Why is feasting or fasting connected to certain holidays?
3. ____ Lin Yutan, a Chinese philosopher, said, "What is patriotism, but the love of good food we ate in our childhood." What do you think it means? Do you agree?

Pair Dictation ❀

Student A will have half of the recipe for Good Luck Dumplings, and will read his/her part to Student B, who has the other half. Student A dictates and Student B writes, then Student B dictates and A writes.

STUDENT B

Good Luck Dumplings

Ingredients

_____ _____ _____, _____, ____ _____, _____ ____ _____ _____.

1/4 teaspoon salt

_____ _____ _____ _____

1 teaspoon minced fresh ginger root

_____ _____ _____

2 tablespoons sesame oil

_____ _____ _____ _____

1 to 2 packages of wonton wrappers

_____ _____ _____ _____

Directions

1. In a large bowl, combine all dumpling ingredients* except wonton wrappers, and mix thoroughly.
2. Wrap about 1 1/2 tablespoons of filling in wonton wrappers. With finger tips, lightly wet edges of wrappers with water. Firmly pinch edges. Repeat until all filling has been used.
3. Place dumplings in slightly salted boiling water, and cook gently for about 10 minutes. Drain; then run cold water over cooked dumplings to avoid sticking.

*If adding vegetables, make sure to blanch them and drain them of excess liquid before combining.

For Soup:
    1 pot of chicken broth, boiling
    Chopped green onions as desired for garnish

1. Add dumplings to boiling chicken broth and cook until done.
2. Garnish with green onions and serve.

Discussion ❀ *Discuss these questions with a partner. Share your ideas with the class.*

1. ____ What special or symbolic foods does your family prepare for your New Year or any other important holiday?

2. ____ Why is feasting or fasting connected to certain holidays?

3. ____ Lin Yutan, a Chinese philosopher, said, "What is patriotism, but the love of good food we ate in our childhood." What do you think it means? Do you agree?

Love Votes *page 156 (CD 1 TRACK 25)*

Introduction

Here are some statements about dating and marriage. Also notice the phrasal verbs that appear in this selection.

Dictation ❀

*After completing the dictation, vote **YES** if you agree with the statement, or **NO** if you disagree.*

Note: *the word "spouse" refers to a husband or wife. The word "mate" in this context means boyfriend or girlfriend.*

VOTE
Yes or **No**

_____

1. You've _____ ____ _____ when someone you *REALLY* like calls you _____ and _____ you _____ for the same night. You try to _____ _____ ____ the first date.

_____

2. You _____ _____ that your spouse is infertile. You really want children of your own and cannot _____ _____. You leave your spouse.

_____

3. Your favorite sister is _____ _____ marry a man who, in your opinion, is _____ _____. She is in love. You try to talk her _____ _____ _____.

_____

4. You have a serious long-distance romance in your country. To relieve _____, you start a romantic _____ locally. You _____ _____ your commitment to the local person.

_____

5. Your teenage daughter is dating a man of another _____. You try to _____ them _____.

_____

6. In order to _____ someone you love, you must _____ _____ your _____ and change to theirs. You do it.

_____

7. You give your mate a gift _____ $200; then you _____ _____ a month _____. You ask _____ _____ _____.

_____

8. You've been _____ ____ _____ a person who loves you much more than you love them. You've been _____ _____ about your feelings but your mate doesn't care. You end the _____ now in order to _____ them a greater _____ later.

Discussion ❀ *Discuss these questions with a partner. Share your ideas with the class.*

1. ____ Do you believe in love at first sight?
2. ____ Would you consider using a computer or newspaper dating service?
3. ____ Would you consider getting married and having only one child?
4. ____ Would you stay with a spouse who is unfaithful? Would it be different if you had three children, or if the "affair" were a one-night stand?
5. ____ How many phrasal verbs can you find in the dictation above?

Independence Day *page 156 (CD 1 TRACK 26)*

Introduction

Until the twentieth century, wars took place mainly in summer, and the War of Independence was no exception. This was partly because most roads were just dirt tracks that turned to deep mud in winter, stopping armies from traveling easily. Armies had to travel at a time of year when there would be plenty of food in the fields to feed the men. Independence Day in the United States is celebrated in July and is the most important patriotic holiday of the year.

Dictation ❀ *There are two columns below, listing the names of countries and their dates of independence. Fill in the blank spaces with the date you hear. With a partner, match the country to the date.*

1. France   a. July 4, 1776

2. United States of America   b. _____

3. Brazil   c. _____

4. Australia   d. _____

5. Canada   e. _____

Discussion ❀ *Discuss these questions with a partner. Share your ideas with the class.*

1. ____ One of the dates above is very different from the others. Why?

2. ____ Does your country have a day when it celebrates its independence? How is it celebrated?

Dictation ❀ *Write the correct word or number in the blank space. Correct and discuss the dictation.*

In this dictation you'll hear about some of the ways the US celebrates its birthday.

_____ _____, the anniversary of the day the Declaration of Independence was signed, is

a day in the United States _____ _____ _____ _____ _____.

About a week before the celebration, you will see small and large flags flying, and stores beginning to

display _____, _____, and _____ _____. In almost every little town

across the country, there is a parade. People line the route _____ _____ _____

_____ _____. The parade often begins with a line of _____ _____

dating from the nineteen twenties and thirties, followed by _____ _____ marching

and playing patriotic songs like "Yankee Doodle Dandy." Even _____ _____ _____ _____

dazzling technology, Americans like to _____ _____ _____ of an old-

fashioned parade.

In the afternoon, friends and family will gather for a

_____ _____ barbecue. At one time, fresh salmon

and fresh peas were part of a _____

_____, but the _____ lends itself to

chicken, steaks, and hot dogs, _____ –

_____ _____ _____.

Everyone waits for dark, _____ _____

_____ _____. Most large cities have extravagant

concerts and firework displays. In Boston, on the Esplanade by the Charles River, _____

_____ _____ will gather to watch and hear the Boston Pops. Some of the crowd

_____ _____ _____ _____ at 6:00 A.M. to get good seats for this great show. The

crowd will _____ _____ to the well-known songs, and a popular star will read the

Declaration of Independence while _____ _____ _____ in the back-

ground. The last piece, Tchaikovsky's 1812 Overture, will include real cannons firing. This is the

traditional ending, and the crowd cheers as the orchestra plays _____ _____ _____. Finally

the moment arrives, and you can hear the crowd's oohs and aahs as the sensational half-hour of

fireworks _____ _____ _____ _____ _____ _____ with red, white, and blue shells that

burst _____ _____ _____ _____ _____ _____ _____.

Discussion ❀ *Discuss these questions with a partner. Share your ideas with the class.*

1. _____ If you celebrate a day of independence in your country, how do you celebrate it?
2. _____ Do you think patriotism is a good thing?
3. _____ These two quotations express different points of view about patriotism. Read and discuss them.

> "I only regret that I have but one life to lose for my country."
> *(Nathan Hale, American Revolutionary patriot)*

> "You'll never have a quiet world till you knock the patriotism out of the human race."
> *(George Bernard Shaw, British author)*

4. _____ Can you think of countries today that are fighting for independence?

Do You Believe in Ghosts? *page 158 (CD 2 TRACK 1)*

Introduction

Do you think that ghosts exist? Do you know anyone who believes in ghosts? Before you do the dictation, talk about the different opinions people in your country have about ghosts.

Dictation ❀ *Write the correct word in the blank space. Correct and discuss the dictation.*

If you'd like to visit some places in the United States that have a reputation _____ _____

_____ , you can buy the book, *The* _____ _____ *of Haunted Places,* by

Dennis Hauck, a well-known _____ on paranormal phenomena. The book contains several

thousand _____ _____ places in countries around the world and mentions many

_____ _____ in the United States.

The most _____ _____ in the White House in Washington, D.C., one that _____

_____ _____ by presidents and their families on many occasions, is _____

_____, the 16th president, who _____ _____ in 1865. Lincoln had many

tragedies_____ _____ _____ _____, one of which was the death of his son,

Willie, at age 11. Lincoln believed _____ _____ _____ and tried several times to

_____ his son through seances in the White House. Lincoln also had _____ of

his own death and once told his secretary that _____ _____ _____ was going to die in office

and that he could _____ his casket in the Rotunda Room of the White House.

Discussion ❀ *Discuss these questions with a partner. Share your ideas with the class.*

1. ____ Have you seen a horror movie? Which one(s)? What was it about?
2. ____ Do you believe that a house can be haunted?
3. ____ Do you believe that mediums can really communicate with the dead?
4. ____ Do you believe that when people die, some part of them can stay with us?
5. ____ Do you believe that some people have really seen ghosts?

6. ____ If ghosts existed, would some be friendly ghosts?

7. ____ Have you ever told a ghost story?

8. ____ Do you enjoy being told such stories?

9. ____ Do you know of any haunted places in your home city or country?

10.____ If you have a good ghost story, tell it to the class!

Discussion ✿ *Read the situation and decide on a response with a partner.*

A woman and her daughter, both teachers, rented a two-bedroom house six months ago. They weren't there long before they realized there was a ghost or spirit living there. At any time of day, lights get turned on and off and doors open by themselves. They are concerned and don't know what to do. Moving out is too expensive and too inconvenient for them right now. Do you have any advice for these educated, sensible women?

Dictation: Judge for Yourself ✿ *Write in the correct words. Correct and discuss the dictation.*

Do you believe that there are people who can tell you the future? People who believe this sometimes go to psychics. These might be palm-readers, fortune-tellers, or tea-leaf readers. In the following court case, Madame Zelda, a psychic, lost her psychic powers.

Madame Zelda was a _____ who _____ she was able to read people's auras and

predict the future. However, after she _____ some tests at the hospital and _____ _____

a CAT scan, she _____ that it _____ her abilities. She _____ that she

was no longer able to read auras, _____ _____ _____, or even help the

police find missing persons as she _____ in the past. Every time she _____ her

psychic powers, she just _____ _____. She _____ the hospital.

Discussion ✿ *Discuss these questions with a partner. Share your ideas with the class.*

1. ____ Do you believe that there are people who can predict the future?

2. ____ Have you ever been (or do you know someone who's been) to a psychic? Tell us about it.

3. ____ Do you think the judge ruled FOR or AGAINST Madame Zelda?

The Verdict ✿ *Write in the correct words. Correct and discuss the dictation.*

The jury _____ _____ Madame Zelda and _____ her _____. However,

the judge, who _____ the final word, _____ the decision and _____ _____ the verdict.

Election Day in the U.S.A. *page 159 (CD 2 TRACK 2)*

Introduction

What do you know about presidential elections in the U.S.? In what month are presidential elections held? How often are presidents elected? How long can presidents serve?

Prediction Dictation ❀

In this activity fill in the blanks before listening to the dictation. Then listen to the same article, write the dictation on the next page, and compare your responses.

In the United States, presidential _____ are held every four years. They are always _____ on the first Tuesday after the first Monday in the month of _____. In most states, Election Day is not a holiday from _____ or school. The President and the Vice-President are _____ for four years. Only natural born _____ of the United States are _____ to be president. Presidents are _____ to be at least thirty-five years old.

There are two major political _____, the Democratic Party _____ the Republican Party. The vice-presidential _____ are selected by the presidential candidates. Both people are nominated by their _____ parties at a national convention several months _____ Election Day.

On Election Day, _____ of Americans go to the polls to _____. Polls are_____ in schools, churches, and public buildings. Polls are _____ from early in the morning until 7:00 or 8:00 in the _____. Most polls use a _____ machine. People always _____ by secret ballot.

Today, all United States _____ 18 and _____ can vote if they want to. In presidential elections, _____ 75% of Americans vote. On election night the votes are tabulated by _____, and the winner is usually _____ by midnight.

Listening Dictation ❀ *Write the correct word in the blank space. Correct and discuss the dictation.*

In the United States, presidential _____ are held every four years. They are always

_____ on the first Tuesday after the first Monday in the month of _____. In most

states, Election Day is not a holiday from _____ or school. The President and the Vice-President

are _____ for four years. Only natural born _____ of the United States are

_____ to be president. Presidents are _____ to be at least thirty-five years old.

There are two major political _____, the Democratic Party _____ the Republican

Party. The vice-presidential _____ are selected by the presidential candidates. Both

people are nominated by their _____ parties at a national convention several months

_____ Election Day.

On Election Day, _____ of Americans go to the polls to _____. Polls are

_____ in schools, churches, and public buildings. Polls are _____ from early

in the morning until 7:00 or 8:00 in the _____. Most polls use a _____ machine.

People always _____ by secret ballot.

Today, all United States _____ 18 and _____ can vote if they want to.

In presidential elections, _____ 75% of Americans vote. On election night the votes

are tabulated by _____ and the winner is usually _____ by midnight.

Discussion ❀

Here is a list of issues that American voters think about before they vote. In Column A, read the issues and check the five <u>you</u> think are the most important. In Column B, do the same for the five issues you think <u>Americans</u> would consider the most important. Compare your answers with others.

COLUMN A	COLUMN B
____ protect the environment	___ protect the environment
____ support abortion	___ support abortion
____ improve education for all	___ improve education for all
____ offer a fair tax system	___ offer a fair tax system
____ balance the federal budget	___ balance the federal budget
____ fight terrorism	___ fight terrorism
____ ensure prosperity	___ ensure prosperity
____ ensure a strong military defense	___ ensure a strong military defense
____ improve the health care system	___ improve the health care system

Discussion ❀

*Interview your teachers and report your findings to the class. Put a check on the line.
Ask: "Which party, Republican or Democrat, is more likely to. . ."*

	Rep.	Dem.
— support abortion rights	____	____
— support gun control	____	____
— support the death penalty	____	____

Discussion ❀

On Election Day, Americans do not vote only for political leaders. They also vote on issues such as taxes and gun control. Here are some political and economic issues that Americans discuss and make decisions on. Look at these issues with your partner and decide if you agree or disagree and give reasons WHY. What issues do you think are most important?

V O T E
For/Against

★ ★ ★ ★ ★ ★ ★ ★ ★ ★ ☆

_____ 1. Change the voting age from 18 to 21 years of age.

_____ 2. Change the legal drinking age from 21 to 18.

_____ 3. Establish one year of mandatory military service for every 18-year-old.
(Right now it's voluntary.)

_____ 4. Establish a law to limit the number of immigrants who can enter the U.S.

_____ 5. Raise taxes to have more money for the military and space programs.

_____ 6. Re-establish the death penalty in all 50 states.

Discussion ❀ *Discuss these questions with a partner. Share your ideas with the class.*

1. ____ Are there any/many women political leaders in your country? Why/why not?

2. ____ What are some different ways leaders are chosen in the world?

3. ____ Are you interested in politics? Why or why not?

The Olympic Games *page 160 (CD 2 TRACK 3)*

Introduction

Every two years, the Winter or the Summer Olympic Games are offered, and they are watched enthusiastically by over 3 billion people around the world. Athletes from many different countries compete in the games. Can you name some famous Olympians from your country? Here is a brief history of the Ancient and Modern Games.

Prediction Dictation ✾

In this activity, fill in the blanks before listening to the dictation. Then listen to the same article, write the dictation on the next page, and compare your responses.

The Ancient Games

Ancient Greece gave birth to the Olympics more than 2000 years _____ in 776 B.C. The Games ended in 394 A.D. During those 1000 years, the Ancient Games _____ festivals to honor the many gods that Greeks _____. Olympia, the town where the most powerful god, Zeus, was worshiped, _____ the first Olympics. The first Olympic Games consisted of no more than _____ foot race, but as the Games _____ more popular, other events were _____, such as horse racing, boxing, chariot racing, and wrestling.

Young men of wealth dominated the early Games, but later, as other sports festivals became more and more popular and offered big cash _____ to winners, men of all _____ of society could make sports a _____ – _____ career. The Olympic Games never offered cash prizes; it was the _____ of winning that meant everything to young men ages 12-17.

The Modern Games

The Olympics were _____ in 1896 and were held every four years. The Modern Games were later _____ into the Winter and _____ Games. Now the Winter and Summer Games alternate every two _____. Fewer countries and sports are represented at the Winter Games because fewer _____ come from countries with high mountains and snow fields. The Summer Games _____ thousands of athletes from over 200 countries and include many more types of sports, _____ _____ swimming and running. Many Olympic athletes today think of the Olympics as more than just _____ the gold, silver, or bronze _____. They _____ that doing your personal best brings respect and understanding for _____ athletes playing the same game for peace _____ humanity.

Listening Dictation ❀ *Write the correct word in the blank space. Correct and discuss the dictation.*

The Ancient Games

Ancient Greece gave birth to the Olympics more than 2000 years _____ in 776 B.C. The Games ended in 394 A.D. During those 1000 years, the Ancient Games _____ festivals to honor the many gods that Greeks _____. Olympia, the town where the most powerful god, Zeus, was worshiped, _____ the first Olympics. The first Olympic Games consisted of no more than _____ foot race, but as the Games _____ more popular, other events were _____, such as horse racing, boxing, chariot racing, and wrestling.

Young men of wealth dominated the early Games, but later, as other sports festivals became more and more popular and offered big cash _____ to winners, men of all _____ of society could make sports a _____ – _____ career. The Olympic Games never offered cash prizes; it was the _____ of winning that meant everything to young men ages 12-17.

The Modern Games

The Olympics were _____ in 1896 and were held every four years. The Modern Games were later _____ into the Winter and _____ Games. Now the Winter and Summer Games alternate every two _____. Fewer countries and sports are represented at the Winter Games because fewer _____ come from countries with high mountains and snow fields. The Summer Games _____ thousands of athletes from over 200 countries and include many more types of sports, _____ _____ swimming and running. Many Olympic athletes today think of the Olympics as more than just _____ the gold, silver, or bronze _____. They _____ that doing your personal best brings respect and understanding for _____ athletes playing the same game for peace _____ humanity.

Discussion ❀

Here is a list of venues for the Modern Games:

2000 Summer Games — Sydney, Australia	11,000 athletes/300 events
2002 Winter Games — Salt Lake City, Utah, USA	2,500 athletes/78 events
2004 Summer Games — Athens, Greece	
2006 Winter Games — Torino, Italy	
2008 Summer Games — Beijing, China	

Decide where you would like to see the Summer and Winter Olympic Games held in 2010, 2012, 2014, and 2016. Discuss the major things to consider when choosing a location.

Winter 2010   _____

Summer 2012 _____

Winter 2014   _____

Summer 2016 _____

Class Contest ❀

Work in groups or 3 or 4 and list as many different events as you can in both the Summer and Winter Olympics. The group with the most correct sports wins the contest. Remember that there are different types of events within sports such as skiing and swimming.

Discussion ❀   *Share your opinions about these sports. Do you enjoy them? Participate?*

swimming	skating	tennis
baseball	basketball	soccer
jogging	table tennis	snowboarding
hockey (field) or (ice)	bicycling	golf
rollerblading	bowling	weight lifting
boxing	rowing	martial arts
gymnastics	hunting	sailing
skiing	wrestling	volleyball
horseback riding	fencing	polo

Birthdays Around the World *page 161 (CD 2 TRACK 4)*

Introduction

The tradition of birthday parties started in Europe a long time ago. It was feared that evil spirits were particularly attracted to people on their birthdays. To protect them from harm, friends and family would come to stay with the birthday person and bring good thoughts and wishes. Giving gifts brought even more good cheer to ward off the evil spirits. In this unit, we will discuss different ways birthdays are celebrated throughout the world today.

Dictation ❀ *Write the correct word or number in the blank space. Correct and discuss the dictation.*

Germany. Germans take birthdays _____, sometimes receiving a _____ – _____ vacation from work. Flowers and wine are _____ _____.

Japan. The birthday child wears _____ new clothes to _____ the occasion. Certain birthdays are more important than others. For example, usually only the birthdays of _____, _____, _____, _____, and _____ rate gifts.

United States. A cake is made, and _____ are _____ _____ _____, based on how old the person is. After everyone sings the "happy birthday" song, the person makes a wish and _____ _____ the candles. If they blow them all out with one blow, their birthday _____ _____ _____ _____.

Denmark. A _____ is _____ outside a window to _____ that someone who lives in that house _____ _____ a birthday. _____ are placed around the _____ _____ while they are sleeping so they will see them _____ _____ _____.

England. When you reach _____, 90, or _____ years of age, you receive a _____ from the Queen. (In the U.S., when you _____ _____, you receive a letter from the _____.)

China. Age _____ is considered _____ an _____, and there is usually _____ _____ _____. Birthdays are traditionally celebrated for adults who _____ _____ at least _____ years of age. Lo mein noodles are often _____.

Mexico. The piñata, usually made out of paper maché and in the _____of an animal, is filled

with _____and hung from the _____. Children _____ _____ hitting the

piñata so candy and small toys _____ _____ for everyone to share. Also, when a

daughter is_____, the birthday is celebrated with a special _____ _____

_____ _____. A party is then given to _____ her to everyone as a young

woman. The father dances a _____ _____ _____.

Ireland. The birthday child is _____ upside down and "_____" on the

floor for good luck. The number of bumps _____ is the age of the child plus one for

_____ _____ _____.

Discussion ❀ *Discuss these questions with a partner. Share your ideas with the class.*

1. _____ If your country is mentioned above, give more information about birthdays. Do you agree
with what is explained here? If not, explain. Is special food prepared? Are there special
gifts or is money given? What birthdays are considered "special"? If your country is not
mentioned above, describe birthday celebrations in your country.

2. _____ In some cultures, birthdays are not celebrated at all. Can you think of any reasons why?

Discussion ❀ *Choose one of the three items below. First, work with a partner, then tell the class.*

1. Talk about what happens when a baby is born in your country.
   - Are most babies born in a hospital, at a clinic, or at home?
   - Do new parents receive cards and gifts? Do the gifts have special significance?
   - Is there a religious ceremony within the first year?
   - Is there a baby shower before the baby is born?

2. Talk about a typical wedding anniversary celebration in your country.
   - Are there parties for special years, such as the 25th or 50th anniversary?
   - Are there special gifts? Do people in your country ever say "no gifts please" on the invitation?
   - Do people take trips instead of having a party?

3. Talk about a typical graduation party in your country.
   - Are there parties for high school and college graduates?
   - Where are the parties held?
   - Do people give gifts? What is a typical gift?

Golden Wedding Anniversary *page 162 (CD 2 TRACK 5)*

Introduction

The Clarks are celebrating their fiftieth (Golden) wedding anniversary. This is an occasion for a party, and all of their sons, their sons' wives, and their grandchildren are coming.

Dictation ❀ *Write the correct word or number in the blank space. Correct and discuss the dictation.*

After doing this dictation, solve this logic puzzle. Put together the name of each husband and wife and how many children they have, where they came from, and when they arrived.

The Clarks were _____ _____ _____ June 20th, when their _____ sons,

and their sons' wives and children were coming to their Utah home for an _____ _____

organized by their son _____. Everyone was _____ to arrive by _____ _____.

Each couple had _____, _____, or _____ children. From the following clues, can

you match the sons with their wives, determine how many children each couple had, _____

their time of _____, and _____ _____ where each family lived?

1. One couple _____ no state or national borders in _____ _____ the homecoming.

2. The couples _____ _____ _____ a t _____, _____, _____,
_____, _____, and _____.

3. The couples from _____ and _____ _____ the same number of children.

4. George _____ only one child, a boy. Eileen has only two girls, and Carol _____ only one girl.

5. The son from _____ _____ at _____ .

6. Pat, who hails from Wyoming, _____ three children and did not arrive either first or last.

7. Frank _____ _____ from _____ and _____ after _____ , two hours after his brother from Japan.

8. Bert and Bob don't _____ the same number of children. The son from Texas _____ one _____ child than the son from Wyoming. The son from Arizona _____ one more child than Frank.

9. Wendy _____ after Jill, who _____ after Linda. But Linda _____ before Eileen, who _____ before _____ .

10. Keith _____ all night and _____ before _____ with his three hungry children.

11. Bert _____ his wife and two children into the car that morning and _____ three hours after Frank.

Discussion ❀ *Discuss these questions with a partner. Share your ideas with the class.*

1. ____ If you were able to solve the problem, share it with your partner or with the class.

2. ____ On what important occasions does your entire family get together?

3. ____ Are there specific names and gifts for special wedding anniversaries in your culture? For instance, in the US, the 25th wedding anniversary is called the "Silver Anniversary," and there is often a big celebration.

4. ____ Do you like this kind of logic puzzle?

You Be the Judge page 163 (CD 2 TRACK 6)

Introduction

Murder and rape are serious crimes. Robbery and assault are somewhat less serious, but the punishment for all crimes has to follow state law. If a murder has been committed in Texas or Florida, for example, the criminal can receive the death penalty. In Massachusetts, the person would go to prison for life. The punishment for manslaughter (accidental killing) also varies from state to state. The judge decides what is fair. In the dictation there are three punishments some criminals actually received. According to public opinion, these punishments were either too strict or too lenient. After taking the dictation, discuss each case and decide what punishment you would approve of.

Dictation ❀ *Write the correct word or number in the blank space. Correct and discuss the dictation.*

Case One. *New York.*

A driver who was _____ down the street at _____ _____ _____ _____ crashed

into a limousine _____ a wedding party. _____ killed were the groom, age 27,

and his brother, age 29, who was the _____ _____. The bride, age 24, died 18 days later

_____ _____ of her husband's death. The driver of the car that killed them

was _____ to _____ years in prison.

Case Two. *Texas.*

A man got into an argument with a police officer and _____ _____ part of the officer's ear.

The man was sentenced to _____ years in prison.

Case Three. *Massachusetts.*

A 14-year-old girl was _____ by a 38-year-old man. She said that her life would never be

the same again. The judge told her to "_____ _____ _____" and sentenced the man to

_____ months in prison.

Discussion ❀ *In a small group, decide on fair punishments for the following crimes. If you think the person should go to jail, decide on how long.*

1. ____ The seriously mentally-ill mother of four boys drowned them in the bathtub. The Texas jury decided that she was guilty and knew what she was doing at the time of the deaths.

2. ____ A Florida man was found guilty of kidnapping and killing a 9-year-old girl who was his next door neighbor. Her mutilated body was found in a field a month later.

3. ____ While driving, a mother of five children in Massachusetts accidentally hit a three-year-old child who ran into the street. She was not speeding. The child died two days later.

Email Spam *page 164 (CD 2 TRACK 7)*

Introduction

If you are a regular email user, no doubt you have received various annoying messages on your computer. These unwanted, unsolicited emails are called spam. Some of these messages are "get rich quick" schemes telling you how you can make lots of money without leaving your home. Others want to help improve the quality of your personal life. Here are two examples.

Dictation ❀ *Write the correct word or number in the blank space. Correct and discuss the dictation.*

1. **Subject:** A Guaranteed University _____!
   From: Educate@COLLdip.741.pm

Do you want to earn the _____ in your _____ that you've always wanted?

You can receive a _____, master's, or doctorate diploma from us and hang it on your

office wall! Our president will _____ accept you through our _____

_____ policy! There are no exams to take, classes to _____, or textbooks to buy.

We award all levels of diplomas from well-known, _____ – _____ universities in any

field of study you wish, including engineering, teaching, computers, _____, or any other

_____. Just call 1-814-453-2312 any time.

2. **Subject:** _____ _____ _____!
   From: Weightloss@diet.761.vn

You can lose one pound a _____ on Dr. Mayer's simple and quick _____ – _____ diet. You

can go from _____ _____ _____ _____ in one week! After the second week on this diet your

clothes will be _____ _____, and you'll have to go out and buy a new _____!

Call today: 1-309-987-8876. Only $_____!

Discussion ❀ *Discuss these questions with a partner. Share your ideas with the class.*

1. _____ If you were curious and decided to call the university diploma group, what questions would you ask?

2. _____ What kind of people would want a bogus diploma hanging on their office wall?

3. _____ What types of scams have appeared on your emails? Have you ever followed through and contacted any of these people? If yes, explain.

4. _____ What warnings would you give to a friend who may be tempted to respond to an email scam?

Questions about Appearance *page 165 (CD 2 TRACK 8)*

Introduction

Do you judge people by their appearance? Are you judged by your appearance? Do you personally care about what you wear and how you look?

Dictation ❀ *Write the correct word or number in the blank space. Correct and discuss the dictation.*

School administrators are girding _____ _____ _____ _____ _____

_____ _____ as racy and revealing back-to-school fashions inspired by navel-baring

pop stars like Christina Aguilera and Britney Spears _____ _____ _____.

_____ _____ _____ _____ have long clashed with adult preferences, principals

say the abundance of skin-revealing styles for girls this year threatens to have _____ _____

_____ _____ _____ _____, _____ _____ _____ _____.

Last year the F.A. Day Middle School in Newton clarified the school's dress code, _____

_____ _____ _____ _____ _____ and _____. But the code is only

a "recommendation" because the school is unclear about _____ _____ _____

_____ _____ _____ _____, said the principal, Paul Stein. The matter,

school officials say, is complicated _____ _____ _____ _____ _____,

First Amendment rights, _____ _____ _____ _____ _____

_____, and the tricky reality that the same outfit may look plain on one girl _____

_____ _____ _____.

Discussion ❀ *Discuss these questions with a partner. Share your ideas with the class.*

1.____ Did you wear a uniform to school? Describe it.
   If you didn't wear a uniform, what did you wear? Were there any restrictions?

2. ____ Should schools have dress codes? Why?

3. ____ Do you believe that the way you dress is a reflection of your personality,
   or is it determined by advertising and peer pressure?

Dictation 2: Judge for Yourself ❀ *Write the correct word in the blank space. Correct and discuss.*

Dress codes can be created by law or by the pressure of society. The following dictation is about a court case concerning a dress code.

In Alaska, a lawyer, _____ _____ _____

_____, was asked by the judge_____ _____

_____ _____ _____ _____ rather than

the more casual attire of a _____ _____

_____ _____ he was wearing. _____ _____

_____ _____ _____ _____ his mode

of dress, he was held in contempt of court. The lawyer

challenged the contempt citation, arguing that it violated

his constitutional right of privacy and liberty _____

_____ _____ _____ _____ ____

_____. Also, _____ _____

_____ _____.

Discussion ❀ *Discuss these questions with a partner. Share your ideas with the class.*

1. ____ Does it make any difference what the lawyer wears? Isn't the only important thing how he pleads the case?
2. ____ Have you ever worked in public? Was there a dress code that you had to follow?
3. ____ What do you think the verdict will be?

The Verdict ❀

The court ruled _____ the lawyer, stating that the court _____ _____ _____ _____

_____ ____ _____ _____ and that a _____ ____ _____ fell within a

_____ _____ ____ _____. _____ _____ _____ _____ _____

_____, the court required women _____ _____ _____ _____

_____, which made _____ _____ _____ _____.

Dictation 3: Judge for Yourself ❀ *Write the correct word in the blank space. Correct and discuss.*

How our hair looks often affects people's perception of themselves. We often grow our hair, cut our hair, shave our hair, curl our hair, straighten our hair, or change our hair color to look better. Here is another case about appearance.

Albert had grown his hair to 10 inches _____ _____ _____ _____ _____ _____. He went to the hair salon bearing a photograph of the style he wanted. _____ _____ _____, _____ _____ _____ because the stylist had cut the hair on top of his head _____ _____ _____. He was ridiculed by his friends and had to resort to _____ ____ _____ _____ _____ _____ _____. He went to a psychiatrist for help. He sued the salon _____ _____ in damages.

Discussion ❀ *Discuss these questions with a partner. Share your ideas with the class.*

1. ____ How annoyed are you in the morning if your hair doesn't look the way you want it to look?
2. ____ Have you ever had a bad experience at a hair salon or barber?
3. ____ How are hair salons or barbers in your country different from the ones in the country you're now living in?
4. ____ Do you think the court ruled "for" or "against" Albert?

The Verdict ❀

The court _____ _____ Albert and _____ the case because the court _____ that the hair _____ _____ _____ _____ _____.

Idioms ❀

How many idioms do you know that are about appearance and clothes? With a partner, discuss the meanings of the following expressions and then discuss them with the class. Can you add several more to the list?

1. _____ She's having a bad hair day.
2. _____ He lost his shirt in the stock market.
3. _____ The train won't be here for another hour, so keep your shirt on.
4. _____ You'd better sock your money away for a rainy day.
5. _____ Last night he tied one on.
6. _____ They're going to tie the knot.
7. _____ The shoe is on the other foot now.
8. _____ He's waiting for the other shoe to drop.
9. _____ She'll go out at the drop of a hat.
10. _____ He's going to throw his hat into the ring.
11. _____ Keep this under your hat.
12. _____ She's just talking through her hat.

Cheating in College *page 166 (CD 2 TRACK 9)*

Introduction

Cheating has always been a problem in high schools and colleges. But now cheating has gotten so sophisticated and so widespread that it's raising serious questions about the integrity of young people and their education.

Dictation ❦ *Write the correct word or number in the blank space. Correct and discuss the dictation.*

1. Cheating in the classroom isn't just about _____ someone's paper or writing answers on a _____ _____. With the _____, cheating has gone _____ _____.

2. _____ of web sites offer _____ papers, class notes, and exams. Students may pay _____ _____ _____ for a research paper bought through the internet.

3. _____ is the most common form of cheating, and university professors admit that it is _____ _____ _____. It depends _____ _____ _____ of faculty members and a certain _____ _____ _____.

4. More than _____ of 2000 students from _____ colleges nationwide _____ _____ _____ last year.

5. Experts say that most students cheat because of _____ _____.

6. _____ on college cheating shows that men and women _____ admitted to _____ dishonesty; business and _____ majors were most likely to cheat, _____ _____ other majors.

7. Colleges are doing more _____ _____ cheating, and universities work with international students who come from _____ that allow _____ another person's work _____ _____ marks or footnotes.

8. At some schools, possible _____ _____ _____ includes _____, but most professors simply give the student an _____ _____ _____ _____.

Discussion ❀ *Discuss these questions with a partner. Share your ideas with the class.*

1. ____ What forms of cheating are common in high schools or universities in your country?
2. ____ Is it more common to find cheating in high schools or in universities?
3. ____ Explain why it is wrong to cheat.
4. ____ Why do students cheat?
5. ____ If the teacher in your country catches someone cheating, what will happen?
   Will the student _____?
       — be given a "zero" on the test
       — be kicked out of school
       — be given a warning
       — be physically punished
       — other?

Discussion ❀ *Discuss these questions with a partner. Share your ideas with the class.*

How honest are <u>you</u>? Decide if the situation is definitely wrong, or if it is "okay."

    Example: You "cheat" on your boyfriend/girlfriend.   *wrong*

1. You tell your teacher you couldn't take the final exam because you were sick. In fact, you were not prepared for the exam because you didn't study all quarter. You ask to take a make-up exam. _____

2. You ask a friend whose English is much better than yours to take the TOEFL test for you. You need a score of 250. You pay him $200. _____

3. You find a wallet with $200 in the school cafeteria. You keep it instead of reporting it to LOST AND FOUND. _____

4. You cheat at a game of cards. _____

5. You sell your 8-year-old car to an interested person. It needs new brakes and the cost of repair is $900. You tell the buyer the car is in excellent condition. _____

6. You are a waiter in a high-class restaurant and make excellent tips. When it's time to fill out your income tax form you report only 70% of what you make. _____

7. You tell your sister that her new baby is beautiful even though the baby is ugly. _____

8. The server in the restaurant forgets to charge you for the extra glass of wine you had. You say nothing. _____

What Would You Do If . . . ? *page 167 (CD 2 TRACK 10)*

Introduction

Sometimes people ask us questions such as, "What would you do if you had a million dollars?" Or "Would you go to the moon for a vacation?" How would you answer? Here are some hypothetical questions for you to practice.

Dictation ❀ *Write the correct word or number in the blank space. Correct and discuss the dictation.*

1. One hot summer afternoon, while _____ _____ a parking lot at a mall, you notice a dog _____ badly from the heat inside a_____ _____. What would you do? Anything?

2. If you went to a dinner party at your _____ house and were _____ some food you had never tried (which looked awful), would you try it _____ _____ it looked _____ or _____ _____?

3. Which sex has _____ _____ _____in your culture, male or female? Have you ever _____ that you were of the_____ _____?

4. You are driving late at night in a safe but _____ neighborhood when a cat suddenly _____ in front of your car. You _____ ____ the brakes, but you hit the cat. Would you stop to see how _____ the cat was? If you did and _____ that the cat was _____ but had a _____ _____, would you _____ _____ _____?

5. Would you ever _____ _____ a week-long vacation _____? If yes, where would you go and what would you do?

6. Would you _____ play a game with someone _____ _____ _____ _____ than you? Why or why not?

7. Would you like _____ _____ _____ some day? Why or why not?

8. If someone _____ you a _____ that made you immortal, would you take it? (The pill is free, has no _____ _____, and could also be given to any _____ _____ people of your _____.)

Discussion ❀ *Discuss these questions with a partner. Share your ideas with the class.*

Who would agree with these statements?

A. Most of my friends   B. My teacher(s)   C. My parents   D. My classmates

1. _____ "Teachers are poorly paid."

2 _____ "American food is terrible."

3. _____ "The classes in this school are too large."

4. _____ "Sometimes it's okay to lie."

5. _____ "Love is more important than money."

6. _____ "It's better to live in the city than in the countryside."

Discussion ❀ *Complete these sentences.*

1. If I had to live in another city, . . .

2. If I had lived a thousand years ago, . . .

3. I would go to Italy if . . .

4. I wish I were on vacation now because . . .

5. I would have bought a car last month if . . .

6. I wouldn't be so tired today if . . .

7. I'll take another English course next semester if. . .

8. If I were Bill Gates, . . .

9. If my landlord raised my rent $100 a month, . . .

10. If the tuition for this school increases 15% next year, . . .

Short Business Decisions *page 168 (CD 2 TRACK 11)*

Introduction

In business there is sometimes a difference between what is legal and what is ethical. There are things that can be done legally, but we know they may not be the right things to do. The following four cases are examples of such situations.

Dictation ❧ *Write the correct word or number in the blank space. Correct and discuss the dictation.*

1. A valuable breakthrough _____ _____ _____ _____ _____ one of your competitors. It is going to improve _____ _____ _____ _____ _____ and reduce _____ _____ _____ _____. Your product will become uncompetitive. Someone comes to you and offers _____ _____ _____ _____ of your competitor's research, which led to his technical breakthrough. _____ _____ _____ _____?

2. Your company has recently acquired _____ _____ _____ _____ as part of the assets of a merger. You are hoping to sign _____ _____ _____ with the local government. You _____ _____ _____ _____ of their chief negotiator _____ _____ and needs to spend the winter in a _____, _____ _____. Do you offer him the use _____ _____ _____ _____ _____ _____?

3. Your company needs _____ _____ _____ _____ _____ for an overseas

   subsidiary. After interviewing the candidates _____ _____ _____, _____ _____,

   is a _____ – _____ – _____ _____. Her husband is a _____ and they have _____

   _____. She is a very valuable member of your staff, and she _____ _____ ___ _____

   that she may leave the company if _____ _____ _____ _____ _____ _____.

   _____ _____ _____ _____, as a woman, she _____ _____ _____ well received

   by the company that she would be working for. This might affect _____ _____ ___ _____

   done by your company. _____ _____ _____ _____?

4. The peak sales time_____ _____ _____ _____ is always in the

   _____ _____ _____ _____. In October you find a _____ _____

   in the product. It is not _____ but _____ _____ the normal life of the

   product. Withdrawing it _____ _____ _____ would mean losing your sales. Would you

   recommend withdrawing it right now?

Discussion ❀ *Discuss these questions with a partner. Share your ideas with the class.*

1. _____ Which of the four situations did you consider the most serious?

2. _____ Do you think there is anything wrong with accepting small favors or small presents from
   people you are dealing with, if you are a government employee?

3. _____ If you are a teacher, is there any problem in accepting a small gift from an appreciative
   student?

Workplace Ethics *page 169 (CD 2 TRACK 12)*

Introduction

Workplace ethics vary from complete honesty (rare) to a little dishonesty (taking paper and pencils and other supplies for personal use) to major dishonesty (stealing money, shredding documents, etc.) Following are a few situations that may test your honesty.

Dictogloss ❀

Listen to a complete sentence only once and write down the words you can remember. With a partner, try to reconstruct the sentence in writing as accurately as possible. When finished, have volunteers write the sentences on the board.

1.

2.

3.

4.

5.

Discussion ❀

With a partner, discuss each of the five situations in the dictogloss and decide what you would do in each situation. Then decide how honest you are.

Dictation: Judge for Yourself ❀ *Write the correct word or number in the blank space.*

Todd was the executor _____ _____ _____ _____ _____

because _____ _____ _____ _____ _____ _____ _____ after his sister

and her husband were killed. _____ _____ _____ _____ and learned of

"a sure thing" in a horserace. He borrowed _____ _____ _____ _____

_____ to place the bet. Todd won _____ _____ _____ _____.

He returned the_____ to the account and kept the rest. _____ what he had done

_____ _____, a friend of his niece helped her sue for the winnings.

Discussion ❀ *Discuss these questions with a partner. Share your ideas with the class.*

1. _____ Was it seriously wrong for Todd to have borrowed the $5000? After all, he returned the
money.

2._____ Did the court rule "For" or "Against" Todd?

The Verdict ❀

The court _____ _____ Todd. _____ _____ did he have

_____ _____ the winnings, _____ the court _____ _____

him of his _____ as an executor for his niece.

What's So Funny? *page 170 (CD 2 TRACK 13)*

Introduction

There are many kinds of jokes and everyone likes to hear a good one. But what is a good joke? One that makes you laugh! Humor is different from culture to culture, and what is funny in one group may not be funny in another. Ethnic jokes poke fun at various nationalities, dirty jokes refer to jokes of a sexual nature. Here are three clean jokes for you to rate according to your personal taste. If you don't understand the joke, you say, "I don't get it." The punch line of a joke is the final sentence that causes you to laugh.

Dictation ❃

Listen and write the word you hear in the blank space. Then, decide if the joke is:
    a. Pretty funny   *b. Not that funny*   *c. Not funny at all*

_____ 1. A woman got on a bus _____ _____ _____. The bus driver said,

"That's _____ _____ _____ I've ever seen." In a huff, the woman

_____ her fare into the fare box and took an _____ seat in the _____ of the

bus. The man _____ next to her sensed that she was _____ and asked

her what _____ _____. "The bus driver _____ _____." The man

_____ and said: "Why, he's a _____ _____ and shouldn't

say things to insult _____." "You're right," she said. "I think I'll go back

up there and give him a _____ of _____ _____." "That's a good idea," the man

said. "Here, let me hold _____ _____."

_____ 2. A guy goes to a psychiatrist because he hasn't been feeling _____ _____. When

the psychiatrist asks him to _____ what is wrong, the guy tells him that he has

been feeling "_____ _____ _____" lately. The psychiatrist then asks

his _____, "How long have you been feeling this way?" The guy _____,

"Ever since I _____ _____ _____."

_____ 3. A person who speaks two languages is _____.

A person who speaks three languages is _____.

A person who speaks four languages is _____.

What is a person who speaks one language? "_____ _____."

Riddles ❀

Read the riddle questions in Column A and with a partner. Then find the correct answer in Column B.

A

1. What is more useful after it's broken?
2. What is worse than finding a worm in an apple?
3. What are two things you can never eat for lunch?
4. What did the woman do when she thought she was dying?
5. What time is it when a lion starts chasing you?
6. If a woman is born in China, grows up in Japan, and dies in the United States, what is she?

B

A. Finding half a worm
B. Time to run
C. An egg
D. Dead
E. Breakfast and dinner
F. She went into the living room

More riddles ❀ *Cover up column B and try to guess the answers.*

A

1. Jenny's parents have 4 kids: Penny, Nickel, and Dime. What's the other kid's name?
2. Who is bigger, Mr. Bigger or his son?
3. I appear once in Tuesday, twice in week, and once in a year. What am I?
4. What 7 letters do you say when you look in the fridge and find no food?
5. Why was 6 afraid of 7?

B

a. Because 7 ate 9
b. OICURMT
c. Jenny
d. The letter E
e. His son because he's a little bigger.

Discussion ❀ *Discuss these questions with a partner. Share your ideas with the class.*

1. _____ Which joke or riddle did you enjoy the most? Why?
2. _____ Are you a good joke teller? Why or why not?
3. _____ What kind of jokes are popular in your country?
4. _____ Can you tell a joke or riddle to the class now?

Try the Internet TESL Journal Web Site at http:/iteslj.org/c/jokes-long.html

Limericks and Tongue Twisters *page 171 (CD 2 TRACK 41)*

Introduction

Limericks are silly poems with five lines that are told in a particular rhyming pattern: AABBA. Listen to the rhythm as your teacher reads it. Then practice saying it aloud with the class.

There once was an odd man named Rod	(A)
Who loved his old car more than God,	(A)
So much that he said	(B)
To his wife, "When I'm dead,	(B)
Bury me in my car on Cape Cod."	(A)

Pair Dictation ❀

Student A will have half of a limerick and will read her/his lines to Student B, who has the other half. Student A dictates and Student B writes; then Student B dictates and A writes until the limerick is complete. When you are finished, practice reciting the limericks.

STUDENT A

1. There once was an old man from Nesser

_____ _____ _____ _____ ____ _____ .

It at last grew so small,

_____ _____ _____ _____ _____

And now he's a college professor!

2. _____ _____ ___ _____ _____ _____ ____

Who loved to go fishing for squid.

____ ____ _____ _____ ____ _____

Who was very defiant,

____ ____ ____ ____ ___ , ____ ___ ____ . (_____ ____ .)

Tongue Twisters ❀ *(see next page)*

Pair Dictation ❀

STUDENT B

Student A will have half of a limerick and will read her/his lines to Student B, who has the other half. Student A dictates and Student B writes; then Student B dictates and A writes until the limerick is complete. When you are finished, practice reciting the limericks.

1. _____ _____ _____ ____ _____ _____ _____ _____

   Whose knowledge grew lesser and lesser.

   ____ _____ _____ _____ ____ _____,

   He knew nothing at all,

   _____ _____ _____ ____ _____ _____!

2. There was a young fellow named Sid

   _____ _____ _____ ____ ____ _____ _____ _____.

   But he caught quite a giant

   _____ _____ _____ _____,

   And ate Sid all up, yes it did. (Poor kid.)

Tongue Twisters ❀

Tongue twisters force you to twist your tongue. Tongue twisters must be said fast — the faster the better. Most tongue twisters need to be repeated a certain number of times. Listen to your teacher and repeat. Then try these with a partner.

Chet chewed two chewy cherries.

Eight apes ate Amy's grapes.

Donna's dogs dig deep ditches.

Frank's frying five fresh fish.

Bella built a beautiful brick building.

Little Ilene lied a lot.

The New World Language   *page 172 (CD 2 TRACK 15)*

Introduction

As a language with many origins — Romance, Germanic, Norse, Celtic, and so on — English is a very messy language. It is also very elastic. New words enter it daily. Nouns become verbs before we know it. It is a language that is always changing — which increases the difficulties for people who are studying it as a second language.

Dictation 1   ❀   *Write the correct word or number in the blank space. Correct and discuss the dictation.*

It is everywhere. _____ _____ _____ _____ it as their first language

and perhaps two thirds as many again as their second. _____ _____ _____ _____

_____. About a third of the world's population are in some sense exposed to it, and by 2050, it is

predicted, _____ _____ _____ _____ _____ _____ _____ _____

proficient in it. It is the language of globalization — of international business, politics, and diplomacy.

It is the language of computers and the internet. You'll see it on posters in Cote d'Ivoire, _____

_____ _____ _____ _____ _____ _____ _____, and you'll read it in

official documents in Phnom Penh. Deutsche Welle broadcasts in it. Bjork, an Icelander, _____

_____ _____. French business schools teach in it. It is the medium of expression in cabinet meetings

in Bolivia. Truly, the tongue spoken back in the _____ only by the "low people" of England

_____ _____ _____ _____ _____. It is now the global language. _____

_____? _____ _____ _____ _____ _____. True, genders are

simple, since English relies on "it" as the pronoun for all inanimate nouns, reserving masculine for

bona fide males and feminine for females (and countries and ships). _____ _____ _____

_____ _____ ____ _____, the grammar bizarre, and the match between _____

and _____ a nightmare. English is now so _____ _____ _____ _____

_____ _____ that umpteen versions have evolved, some so peculiar that "native"

speakers may have trouble understanding each other.

Discussion ❀

Do you agree or disagree with these statements?

1. ____ English is an easy language to learn.
2. ____ English is an easier language to learn than my first language.
3. ____ American English is very different from British English.
4. ____ There are many similarities between English and my first language.

Dictation 2 and Pronunciation ❀

In English we have some words that are spelled the same but are pronounced differently and generally have different meanings. Here is an example: "We polish the Polish furniture." In the first part of the sentence, "polish" is a verb and means to rub something to make it clear and shiny. The second "Polish" is the adjective identifying something or someone as being from Poland, a country in Europe. Fill in the blank spaces with the word or words you hear. Repeat the sentences after your teacher says them.

1. They are too _____to the door to _____it.

2. There was a _____among the oarsmen about how to _____.

3. I shed a _____about the _____in my new shirt.

4. A farm can _____ _____.

5. The dump was so full it had to _____ _____.

6. The_____is a good time to_____ the_____.

7. The insurance for the _____was _____.

8. The bandage was _____ around the _____.

9. The soldier decided to _____ in the _____.

Discussion ❀ *Discuss these questions with a partner. Share your ideas with the class.*

1. ____ Can you think of similar pairs of words in English?
2. ____ Can you think of other words that cause pronunciation problems in English?
3. ____ Can you think of something in your own language that would cause confusion for someone studying your language?

Dictation 3 ❀ *Write the correct word or number in the blank space. Correct and discuss the dictation.*

An international exchange student _____ _____ _____ _____ _____ _____

_____ _____ _____ at a party. He is confident in his ability to hold a conversation

with everyone, _____ _____ _____ _____ _____ _____. Then someone

offers one of his friends a drink. The friend replies, "Um, like no, I'm like OK." The student thinks,

"_____ _____ _____ _____ _____."

Slang and filler speech is so ingrained in _____ _____ _____. The

word "like" has infiltrated so many young minds that no sentence is left untouched by these

"non-fluencies."

_____ _____ _____ _____ _____. _____ _____ _____, California's

"valley-girl" talk has plagued America's youth _____ _____ _____ _____.

_____ _____ Professor Richard Katula of Northeastern University's communications

studies department, these filler words allow teenagers who feel vulnerable expressing their beliefs a

"way out."

He translated the use of "like" as "what I just said, I may not mean." These filler words are referred

to as negative speech, _____ _____ _____ _____ _____. Those interjected

"likes" give unsure youths a moment to soften or manipulate what could have otherwise been a

strong, personal, confrontational statement. Often the result is _____ _____ _____

_____ _____ _____.

Discussion ❀ *Discuss these questions with a partner. Share your ideas with the class.*

1. ____ Have you heard many people using "like" as a filler word?
2. ____ Do people do something similar in your language?
3. ____ Have you learned many slang expressions since you began studying English?
   What are some of these?

Trivia Contest   *page 174 (CD 2 TRACK 16)*

Introduction

A contest is a game with winners and losers. Trivia is defined as information that is not important but is often fun to know.

Dictation   ❀

After you fill in the blank spaces, work together in groups of three quietly so other groups don't hear your answers and answer as many questions as you can. Guess if you don't know. Assign one person as secretary to write down your answers. Your teacher will come around to each group to get your answers. The group with the most correct answers wins!

1. How many people are there in _____ _____?

2. Where are most American cars _____ in the U.S.?

3. _____ _____ are presidential _____ _____ in the U.S?

4. Who wrote *The _____ of Huckleberry _____*?

5. What does ____ ____ ____ mean? (**Hint:** *it's a kind of sandwich*)

6. Where can you buy a _____ _____?

7. Who is the _____ _____ in the world?

8. In what year did Americans _____ _____ on the moon?

9. What is the _____ _____ first name in the world? (**Hint:** *it's not an American name*)

10. What is the _____ – _____ ice cream _____ in the U.S.?

11. How long has your teacher _____ in this program?

Discussion: A Quiz for your Teacher!   ❀

Work in groups of three. Make up questions about students in your class or about your school that you think your teacher can answer but may have forgotten. Practice using questions with: "Do you know . . . ?" "Can you remember . . . ?"

Here are a few sample questions:

1. How long has (a classmate) been in the United States?

2. What is (a classmate's) major?

3. When was this school founded?

Who Would Say That? *page 175 (CD 2 TRACK 17)*

Introduction

Sometimes you overhear a conversation and guess what people are talking about. In this dictation, guess who's talking.

Dictation ❀ *In some cases, more than one answer is possible.*

Example: "These tee shirts only come in size large."   **Answer:**   *Store clerk*

1. "It's a l999 and in perfect _____. And it only has

   _____ miles."   _____

2. "Do you have any _____ _____?"   _____

3. "We expect to be _____ _____ in about ten minutes."   _____

4. "I think that "Snoopy" should go _____ _____ _____."   _____

5. "Ugga mugga hubba _____ goolak."   _____

6. "Would you like to try something different this time? A _____?

   Or a _____?"   _____

7. "I _____that next year you'll meet the perfect man and get

   _____."   _____

8. "It's a _____ _____ for Reggie. Now it's _____

   two to two."   _____

9. "May I see your driver's license and _____, please?" _____

10. "It's a beautiful _____ _____ two-bedroom."   _____

11. "_____ _____"   _____

12. "The _____ is 10 cents a day for each one that is _____." _____

Exercises ❀

1. _____   After completing the dictation, in pairs or small groups, try saying all of the quotes above as indirect quotes, for example, The store clerk said (that) those teeshirts only came in size large.

2. _____   With a partner, make up some quotes of your own and let the class guess "who said it."

Don't Be Fooled! *page 176 (CD 2 TRACK 18)*

Introduction

Here are some tricky questions. Don't be fooled! But don't worry, you won't look foolish!

Dictation ✿ *After checking the dictation, try to figure out the answer with a partner.*

*Example: Which is correct to say, "The yolk of an egg **are** white" or "The yolk of an egg **is** white?"*
Answer: Neither. The yolk of an egg is yellow!

1. Mary Jones was born on December 27th, _____ her birthday is always _____ _____ _____.
   How can this be?

2. Frank was walking down Main Street when it started to _____. He did not have an umbrella
   and he wasn't wearing a hat. His clothes _____ _____, yet not a hair on his head _____
   _____. How could this happen?

3. There is an _____ _____ still used in parts of the world today that _____
   people to see through _____. What is it?

4. A taxi driver took a group of _____ to the train station. The station is _____ an
   hour away, but with terrible traffic, it took a full hour and _____ _____. On the return trip, the
   traffic was still as _____ and yet it took only _____ minutes. Why?

5. Do they have a 4th of July _____ _____?

6. Some months have _____ days; others have 31 days. How many have _____ days?

7. What five-letter-word becomes _____ when you add _____ _____ to it?

8. A farmer had _____ _____. _____ _____ _____ died. How many did he have left?

9. A woman from New York _____ ten different men from that city, yet she didn't _____
   _____ _____. None of the men _____ and she _____ _____. How
   was this possible?

10. Which one of the following words _____ _____ _____ with the _____ and why?
   Father, Aunt, Sister, _____, Mother, Uncle.

Riddles

A
1. What is the longest word in the English language?
2. What has arms and legs but no head?
3. What never asks questions but gets many answers?
4. How many 37-cent stamps are there in a dozen?

B
a. a chair
b. a doorbell
c. twelve
d. smiles (because there's a mile between both s's)

Learning Styles *page 177 (CD 2 TRACK 19)*

Introduction

How many ways are there to learn? According to several psychologists, there are seven specific types of learning styles: Linguistic, Logical, Spatial, Musical, Bodily, Interpersonal, and Intrapersonal. An important factor in understanding learning styles is understanding brain functioning. Both sides of the brain can reason, but by different strategies, and one side may be dominant. The left-brain is considered analytic in approach, while the right is described as holistic or global.

Dictation ❀ *Write the correct word or number in the blank space. Correct and discuss the dictation*

Here is a description of one type of learner, _____ _____ _____. These children

are very mathematically inclined. _____ _____ _____, particularly if they

are _____ _____. They are _____ _____ Mr. Spock on "Star Trek," in

that they are very logical, straightforward types of learners. They will plague you with questions

_____ _____ _____ _____, how things relate to one another, and

_____ _____ _____ _____. Their _____ _____ as young children

were building blocks and pattern puzzles. _____ _____ _____ _____

with as much patience as you can muster, and one day they may become engineers.

_____ _____ _____ _____ _____ _____ _____ _____ _____

_____ _____, psychologists will give you a learning style inventory test. Here are some

examples of the type of question you may be asked. Check the statements that are true about you.

_____ I prefer to _____ with things while I listen or talk to people.

_____ I prefer to _____ _____ _____ rather than listen to someone giving me directions.

_____ I _____ a lot when I explain things.

_____ I enjoy doing more _____ _____ _____ ____ _____ _____.

_____ I often _____ while I study.

_____ When I read, _____ _____ _____ and try to "feel" the content or even act

out parts of what I read.

Discussion ❀ *Discuss these questions with a partner. Share your ideas with the class.*

Compare your answers to the questions above with those of another person. Can you determine what kind of learners you are?

Test

Do the following short learning style inventory test to determine if you are an Auditory Learner or a Visual Learner. Write A or V in the space.   **A or V**

1. I would prefer to
   follow a set of oral directions. (auditory)
   follow a set of written directions. (visual)   _____

2. I would prefer to
   attend a lecture given by a famous psychologist. (auditory)
   read an article written by a famous psychologist. (visual)   _____

3. I am better at
   remembering names. (auditory)
   remembering faces. (visual)   _____

4. It is easier to learn new information
   using language. (auditory)
   using images. (visual)   _____

5. I prefer classes in which the instructor
   lectures and answers questions. (auditory)
   uses films and videos. (visual)   _____

6. To obtain information about current events I would prefer to
   watch TV news. (auditory)
   read the newspaper. (visual)   _____

7. To learn how to use a fax machine, I would prefer to
   go to a demonstration. (auditory)
   Consult a manual. (visual)   _____

Score: Auditory _____ **Visual** _____
A score of 4 to 3 in this might indicate a tendency toward being one kind of learner or another; obviously, greater differences in a score show such a tendency even more clearly.

Auditory or Visual: This score indicates the sensory mode you prefer when processing information. Auditory learners tend to learn more effectively through listening while visual learners process information by seeing it in print or other visual modes, including film, picture, or diagram. If you have a higher score on auditory than visual you tend to be an auditory learner. That is, you tend to learn more easily by hearing than by reading.

Discussion   ❀   *Discuss these questions with a partner. Share your ideas with the class.*

1. ____ Do you think that the schools you went to affected your learning style?

2. ____ How can your learning style relate to your study of English?

Test

Take another short learning style inventory test to see if you're a social learner or an independent learner. Write S or I in the space.   **S or I**

1. For a grade in biology lab, I would prefer to
    work with a lab partner. (social)
    work alone. (independent)   _____

2. When faced with a difficult personal problem, I prefer to
    discuss it with others. (social)
    resolve it myself. (independent)   _____

3. Many instructors could improve their classes by
    including more discussion and group activity. (social)
    giving students more time to work by themselves. (independent)   _____

4. When listening to a lecture or speaker, I respond more to
    the person presenting the ideas. (social)
    the ideas themselves. (independent)   _____

5. When on a team project, I prefer
    to work with several team members. (social)
    to divide up tasks and complete those assigned to me. (independent)   _____

6. I frequently try to shop, run errands, and work with friends. (social)   _____
    I seldom try to shop, run errands and work with friends. (independent)

7. A job in a busy office is
    more appealing than working alone. (social)
    less appealing than working alone. (independent)   _____

Score: Social ____ Independent____

A score of 4 to 3 in this might indicate a tendency toward being one kind of learner or another: obviously, greater differences in a score show such a tendency even more clearly.

This score reveals your preferred level of interaction with other people in the learning process. If you are a social learner, you prefer to work with others — both other students and instructors. If you are an independent learner, you prefer to work and study alone; you tend to be self-directed or self-motivated, and you are often goal oriented.

Discussion   ❀   *Discuss these questions with a partner. Share your ideas with the class.*

1. ____ If you have studied in more than one country, were there differences in classroom teaching that affected your learning style?

2. ____ Are there any advantages in knowing what your learning style is?

What Used To Be *page 178 (CD 2 TRACK 20)*

Introduction

When we talk about the present and how different it is today from the past, we usually use "used to."

Dictation - Part A ❀

Fill in the blanks with the word or words you hear. Then, with a partner, check your dictation and find the answers to the incomplete sentences in Part B.

Example: Before electricity, people used to . . . read by candlelight.

1. Before _____, people used to . . .

2. The country that is now called _____. . .

3. Before _____ _____, people used to. . .

4. _____ of years ago. . .

5. Before doctors became _____ , _____ used to. . .

6. In many _____ and not so ancient cultures, . . .

7. Before the car was _____ people used to . . .

8. The country that _____ _____ _____ called Ceylon . . .

9. People used to think that _____ . . .

10. Before _____, people used to . . .

Part B ❀

Use these phrases to complete the sentences in Part A above. There are two extra ones here!

perform some operations	is now called Sri Lanka	travel by horse
were poisonous	people didn't use to travel by plane	read more
used to be called Siam	women never used to wear blue jeans	use typewriters
people used to have slaves	dinosaurs used to roam the earth	read by candlelight

Discussion ❀

1. _____ I used to . . . but now. . .
2. _____ My parents used to . . . . but now. . .
3. _____ People in my country . . . but now . . .

All About Weather *page 179 (CD 2 TRACK 21)*

Introduction

If you live in an area where weather is constantly changing, weather is probably one of the topics that people speak about all the time, both to strangers and to friends. In many areas, the three main topics of conversation are politics, sports, and the weather. This is not so unusual since weather plays a major role in our daily lives.

Pair Dictation ✤

Student A will have half of the weather jokes and will read her/his part to student B, who has the other half. Student A dictates, and student B writes; then Student B dictates, and Student A writes until each joke is finished. With your partner, correct the dictation and decide which joke you think is funnier.

STUDENT A

Joke 1. I had just moved north _____ _____ _____ _____ about the severity

of the winters. My anxious questions _____ _____ _____ brought this reply

from a native. "_____, _____ _____ _____ _____ _____: early

winter, _____, late winter, _____ _____ _____."

✶✶✶✶✶✶✶✶✶✶✶✶✶✶✶✶✶✶✶✶✶✶✶✶✶✶✶✶✶✶✶✶✶✶✶✶✶

Joke 2. The Michaels family owned _____ _____ _____ _____ _____

just yards away from _____ _____ _____ _____. Their land had been

the subject _____ _____ _____ _____ between Canada and the United States

_____ _____. Mrs. Michaels, _____ _____ _____ _____

_____ _____ _____, lived on the farm _____ _____ _____ _____

_____ _____. One day, her son came into her room _____ _____

_____. " I just got some news, Mom," _____ _____. "_____ _____

has come to an agreement _____ _____ _____ _____ _____. They've

decided that our land _____ _____ _____ _____ _____ _____

_____. We have the right to approve or disapprove _____ _____ _____.

What do you think?" "_____ _____ _____ _____ ?" _____ _____ _____.

"Jump at it! _____ _____ _____ _____ and tell them we accept. _____

_____ _____ _____ _____ _____ another one of those Canadian winters."

Pair Dictation ❦

Student A will have half of the weather jokes and will read her/his part to student B, who has the other half. Student A dictates, and student B writes; then Student B dictates, and Student A writes until each joke is finished. With your partner, correct the dictation and decide which joke you think is funnier.

STUDENT B

Joke 1. _____ _____ _____ _____ _____ and was feeling apprehensive _____

_____ _____ _____ _____ _____ . _____ _____ _____ about the

weather _____ _____ _____ _____ _____ _____ . "Ma'am, we have

four seasons here: _____ _____ , midwinter, _____ _____ , and next winter.

✳✳✳✳✳✳✳✳✳✳✳✳✳✳✳✳✳✳✳✳✳✳✳✳✳✳✳✳✳✳✳✳✳✳✳

Joke 2. _____ _____ _____ _____ a small farm in Canada _____ _____

_____ _____ the North Dakota border. _____ _____ _____ _____ _____

_____ of a minor dispute _____ _____ _____ _____ _____

_____ for generations. _____ _____ , who had just celebrated her ninetieth

birthday, _____ _____ _____ _____ with her son and three grandchildren. _____

_____ , _____ _____ _____ _____ _____ _____ holding a letter. "_____

_____ _____ _____ _____ , _____ ," he said. "The government _____

_____ _____ _____ _____ with the people in Washington. _____

_____ _____ _____ _____ is really part of the United States. _____ _____

_____ _____ _____ _____ _____ _____ of the agreement. _____

_____ _____ _____ ?" "What do I think?" his mother said. "_____ _____ _____!

Call them right now _____ _____ _____ _____ _____ . I don't think I could

stand _____ _____ _____ _____ _____ _____ ."

Dictation 2 ✽

The following are just a few of the many weather expressions in the English language.

1. It was a _____ _____ of precipitation.

2. It's raining _____ _____ _____.

3. I'll take _____ _____ _____.

4. Don't rain _____ _____ _____.

5. I can _____ the storm.

6. I'm _____ _____ _____.

7. It was a real _____ _____.

8. I was _____ _____ with work.

9. The problems _____ by the hour.

10. I was _____.

11. The idea came _____ _____ _____ _____.

12. She was _____ _____ _____.

13. Her head was _____ _____ _____.

Discussion ✽ *Discuss these questions with a partner. Share your ideas with the class.*

1. _____ What is the climate like in your country?

2. _____ Which climate would you prefer to live in, one that has four seasons — summer, autumn, winter, and spring — or one that is pleasantly warm and sunny, 365 days a year?

3. _____ How does climate affect the economy? What are the economic advantages and disadvantages of living in a warm or cold climate?

4. _____ What is the worst weather you've ever experienced?

5. _____ How does weather affect your mood?

Facts About Drinking *page 180 (CD 2 TRACK 22)*

Introduction

What is the legal drinking age in your state? Is underage drinking common in your community? Is drunk driving a problem where you come from? How much do you know about drinking? Talk about these questions and then try the dictation and decide if the statement is true or false.

Dictation ❀ *Write the correct word or number in the blank space. Correct and discuss the dictation.*

_____ 1. Some people can drink a lot without _____ _____ drunk.

_____ 2. Approximately 40% of _____ highway accidents are _____ _____ .

_____ 3. _____ _____will make you drunker than staying with one kind of alcohol.

_____ 4. You can _____ _____ _____with milk or food to slow down the rate

of intoxication.

_____ 5. The best way to _____ _____ is to drink coffee and take a cold shower.

_____ 6. _____ experts say that one out of every two Americans will _____

_____ ____ a drunk driver.

_____ 7. A person _____ _____ on alcohol.

_____ 8. It is easy _____ _____ an alcoholic.

_____ 9. Drinking during pregnancy can affect the _____ _____ .

____ 10. Most alcoholics are _____ – _____ or older.

____ 11. Children of alcoholics are _____ _____ to develop alcoholism.

____ 12. _____ _____ is defined as 5 drinks _____ _____ _____

for men and _____ drinks within an hour for women.

____ 13. A _____ _____ is someone who drinks 4-5 drinks every night.

____ 14. All drinkers are _____ _____ .

____ 15. _____ _____account for 25% of the alcohol consumed in the United States.

Discussion ❀

Charles Dixon was arrested for drunk driving last year in Boston. No accident happened but this was the second time the police had stopped him. His license was taken away for 6 months; he was fined $1000 and ordered to attend an alcohol-education program. Do you think this punishment was fair? Why or why not?

What kind of punishment should these people get?

    A. a warning   **B.** go to jail – how long?   **C.** pay a fine – how much?

    D. take away the license – how long?   **E.** attend an alcohol-education program

1. _____ A woman was driving drunk. She was speeding and driving recklessly. No accident happened and this was her first offense. She was 19 years old.

2. _____ A man, age 50, was driving drunk and hit another car. The people in that car were not seriously injured but had to go to the hospital by ambulance for examination.

3. _____ A drunk woman, age 22, hit another car. The person in the other car died.

Discussion ❀ *Discuss these questions with a partner. Share your ideas with the class.*

1. _____ The attitude toward drinking is different in every country. Talk about the attitude toward drinking in your culture.

2. _____ Car insurance in the U.S. is very expensive for drivers under the age of 25. Discuss why.

3. _____ Imagine a close friend has a hangover. He has to take an exam in two hours. You want to help him. Talk about the following possibilities and one or two good solutions.

    take 3 Extra-strength Excedrin   call the professor and tell her the situation

    continue drinking alcohol   don't take the test but e-mail the professor

    drink a lot of coffee   your suggestion

Increasing Birth Size *page 182 (CD 2 TRACK 23)*

Introduction

Bigger babies are the outcome of positive changes in many cultures. Women are encouraged to stop smoking, allowing healthier development of the fetus, and they are under less pressure to stay slender while pregnant. But how big is too big?

Dictogloss

Listen to a complete sentence only once and write down the words you can remember. With a partner try to reconstruct the sentence in writing as accurately as possible.

1.

2.

3.

4.

Discussion   ❀   *Discuss these questions with a partner. Share your ideas with the class.*

1. ____ How much did you weigh when you were born? In kilograms? _____ In pounds _____ ?
2. ____ If you're a woman, are you taller than your mother? If you're a man, are you taller than your father? What do you think the reasons for this may be?

Dictation   ❀   *Write the correct word or number in the blank space. Correct and discuss the dictation.*

"_____ _____ _____ evolution, we are in a _____ _____ _____,"

said James Boster, an anthropologist at the University of Connecticut. _____ _____

_____ _____ _____ babies were born in primitive conditions. But _____

_____ _____ died in childbirth. Now with access to _____ _____ _____,

the previous consequences of having babies _____ _____ _____ _____ are remedied

surgically.

_____ _____ _____ _____ _____, growth has been dramatic. In 1760, Norwegian soldiers averaged _____ _____ _____. American soldiers drafted for World War I averaged _____ _____ _____ _____ _____. Today the average Californian male is _____ _____ _____ inches and weighs _____ _____.

_____ _____ _____ _____ _____ is how much larger people will grow. To project _____ _____ _____ _____ _____, anthropologists look to the past. _____ _____ _____ _____ _____ _____ our African ancestors stood _____ _____ _____ _____, according to Daniel Lieberman, a professor at Harvard University. But as early humans moved from a hunter-gatherer society to agriculture, food variety _____, disease _____, and people migrated _____ _____ _____ — favoring shorter, squatter physiques — and _____ _____ _____ _____ all these factors, heights shrank. It is only _____ _____ _____ _____ _____ that humans have begun to play catch-up. They haven't peaked yet, but they are getting close. In the Netherlands (_____ _____ _____ _____ _____ _____ _____ _____) the average height of the men is _____ _____ _____ _____ _____. It appears that genetics won't allow humans to get much bigger.

The difference between men and women, which has been shrinking _____ _____ _____ _____ may some day disappear, anthropologists say. _____ _____ _____ _____ men were _____ _____ _____ _____. Between 30,000 and 50,000 years ago men and women grew noticeably _____ _____ _____. Today, height differences _____ _____. The gender gap is directly related to mating habits, scientists say. The more polygamous a species, the greater the size differential between men and women.

Discussion ❀ *Discuss these questions with a partner. Share your ideas with the class.*

1. ____ Do you think that there are advantages to being tall? to being short?
2. ____ Have you ever wished that you were taller or shorter?
3. ____ (For men) Would it matter to you if your girlfriend or wife were taller than you?
4. ____ (For women) Would it matter to you if you were taller than your boyfriend or husband?

Nutrition and Obesity *page 184 (CD 2 TRACK 24)*

Introduction

How much do you know about your general health and nutrition? Here are some statements that may surprise you!

Dictation 1: Nutrition ❀

First, listen and write the word you hear in the blank space. Then, work with a partner and decide if the statement is true or false.

_____ 1. Low-fat milk has more _____ _____ _____ milk.

_____ 2. Multivitamin pills can give you _____ _____.

_____ 3. It's better to eat a _____ _____ and a smaller dinner.

_____ 4. People who do not eat meat, fish, or chicken are _____ _____ _____ _____ those who do.

_____ 5. Fresh vegetables are always _____ _____ _____ frozen.

_____ 6. If you want to make one _____ in your diet, _____ _____ on fat would be better _____ _____ less often.

_____ 7. A glass or two of wine _____ _____will help you sleep well.

_____ 8. _____ helps keep you in good _____.

_____ 9. When you're _____ ___ _____, it's better to drink white wine _____ ____.

_____ 10. You've been asked to _____ _____ _____. A good serving size would be _____ _____ _____ ____ a deck of cards.

_____ 11. Butter contains _____ _____ _____ _____.

_____ 12. Women who eat at least _____ servings of fruits and vegetables _____ reduce their _____ of diabetes by _____.

Dictation 2: Obesity ❀

Write the right word in the blank space. Correct and discuss the dictation.

Despite a seeming obsession with their health, _____, and _____, Americans are getting

_____ _____ _____. New information shows that more than half of all _____ in

the U.S. are _____, and the number of obese people — defined _____ _____ _____

over the ideal weight — increased from _____ in 1991 to _____ in 1998.

Researchers say they are _____ _____ how fast Americans are _____ extra

pounds, and some say that _____ — which perhaps kills as many as _____

_____ _____ — should be considered a real public health problem and not simply a

_____ one.

Dr. George Blackburn, director of the division of _____ at Beth Israel Deaconess Medical

Center, said that _____ _____ _____ 15 years, Americans have become aware that diet and

exercise can _____ _____ for many health complications, such as high blood _____,

heart disease, or diabetes, but they just _____ _____ to do it yet.

"Fewer people are doing what they know they should do. _____, everybody just wants

a _____ _____," Blackburn said. "But they don't _____ if they can spend

an extra few minutes _____ _____ , and as little as 200 _____ less a day, they

would be _____ _____ lighter by the end of the year."

Two reasons why Americans are _____ weight are easy to _____:

   (1) They _____ _____ in restaurants at least _____ _____ _____ times a week.

   (2) They _____ _____ a health club, but after 6 months _____ of them quit.

Discussion ❀ *Discuss these questions with a partner. Share your ideas with the class.*

1. How does the diet of your country compare with the American diet?

2. Has the diet of the people in your country changed in the past 10 or 20 years?

3. Do you know of any markets in your city here in the U.S. or at home that sell only organically grown food? Why is this important to some people?

4. 800,000,000 people in the world are underfed. Can you give two reasons for this?

Exercise *page 186 (CD 2 TRACK 25)*

Introduction

Do you exercise regularly? Do you think about exercising regularly? Do you make resolutions about exercising regularly? The following dictogloss and dictation will give you some good reasons to begin.

Dictogloss

Listen to a complete sentence only once and write down the words you remember. Then try to reconstruct the sentence. Finally, decide whether it is "True" or "False" and why.

1.

2

3.

4.

5.

Dictation ❀ *Write the correct word or number in the blank space. Correct and discuss the dictation.*

The following dictation is from an obituary (a death notice), and it is about an unusual jogger.

Ruth Rothfarb of Cambridge was an_____ _____who _____many

by _____ in the Boston _____ (26 miles), the Tufts 10K (10 kilometers), and other

long- distance races.

Mrs. Rothfarb, who_____Wednesday at age _____, began running at the age of

_____. She began running competitively a few years later.

She _____in several Boston _____and Tufts 10K races _____ _____

_____ long-distance races in Atlanta, Los Angeles, New Zealand, and Thailand before her

retirement from _____ running at the age of _____.

She was born in Russia and _____ to the United States as a teenager in _____.

After her marriage, she _____full-time maintaining a home, raising two children, and helping her husband _____the family clothing business.

At the age of _____ she found herself with_____ _____ _____ _____ after her husband _____, their business was sold, and her children were _____. "I had to do something," she said. "I wasn't going to sit around doing nothing."

She began taking walks _____ the Charles River and _____ Fresh Pond. When the jogging _____ came to her neighborhood, she _____ up her speed. "If they can do it, I can _____," she said. "It's simple enough. All you have to do is pick up your feet and go."

In _____, she accompanied her son, Herbert, to a ten-kilometer race. "While everyone was _____ _____, I asked my son if they'd laugh at me if I ran," she said. "He said 'no.' So I ran. And I finished. It took me a long time, but I finished." She was _____ at the time.

At the age of _____ she was running about _____ miles a day and running _____ in about _____ hours. "I like to _____ _____," she said. "If I feel like doing something, I want to do it. I don't want to have to wait around for anybody else. I don't believe in spending afternoons just sitting around having tea. I do things."

Discussion ❀ *Discuss these questions with a partner. Share your ideas with the class.*

1. ____ Is jogging popular in your country? Who jogs? (ages, classes, males, females) Where do people jog? What do they wear?

2. ____ When very old people are asked what they think contributed to their long life span, they might answer that a daily glass of wine was the reason for their reaching 100. What do you think Ruth Rothfarb would answer?

3. ____ Can you think of any negative effects of exercise?

4. ____ Are you satisfied with the amount of exercise you do?

How's Your Mental Health? *page 188 (CD 2 TRACK 26)*

Introduction

Mental health issues affect large numbers of people not only in the United States but all over the world. Years ago, mental illness was not discussed in public, as if it were a deep, dark, shameful secret to be kept only within the family. Nowadays, with more information and research about different mental illnesses, people can educate themselves about the nature of these illnesses and learn how to get the right kind of help for themselves, a family member, or friend, when it is needed.

Dictation   ❀   *Write the correct word or number in the blank space. Correct and discuss the dictation.*

The Surgeon General of the United States recently _____ that _____ in _____ Americans

suffers from a _____ illness. Although some may feel this is overstated, imagine that:

- _____ in _____women will experience _____ depression in their lives, as

   will _____ in _____men.

- Eight to twelve percent of the population experiences a significant _____ _____.

- _____ in _____children has attention deficit hyperactivity disorder (ADHD).

- One percent of the population has _____ depression or bipolar illness.

- _____ percent of the population has schizophrenia.

Through education and information it is important to be able to look at depression, anxiety, ADHD,

and sleep _____ not as _____ but rather as real and medically based illnesses.

Considering mental health problems to be _____ – _____based means that far too many

will go unrecognized and _____.

The _____ _____mental illness is depression. Different forms of depression

_____ from short-term, low mood after a _____ life experience to an

_____ form of depression linked to decreased energy, interest, and _____

along with changes in appetite and sleep — called _____ _____.

Depression may also take place in women following _____ as well as in people during

certain _____of the year. Being unable to perform at work, having little wish to

_____, and becoming _____from family members may all take place during

depression. Depression very much needs to be viewed as a _____ illness and not as a

weakness. Recognizing and treating depression not only _____ life but also _____ lives.

Discussion   ❀   *Discuss these questions with a partner. Share your ideas with the class.*

1. ____ Low-mood depression is steadily increasing among students. In some schools there is a 40% increase in the need for counseling sessions. Here are a few reasons why. Which do you think are the most serious? Can you think of any other reasons?

- fitting in
- academic pressure/ meeting expectations
- finding a career
- adjusting to a new place/ homesickness
- fear of war/bio-terrorism
- financial woes

- sexual orientation
- forming relationships
- information overload
- long-term abuse
- problems at home (family/ economic/political)
- bereavement
- your reasons

2. ____ More serious forms of depression are often treated with medication, once the diagnosis has been made. Prozac and other anti-depressant drugs are commonly used and allow sufferers to live a fairly "normal" life. What other mental illnesses mentioned in the dictation do you think would most likely require medication? Why?

3. ____ Universities, especially those with high suicide rates, have been forced to make a major overhaul of their mental health services. Here are some changes that are taking place throughout the United States. In small groups or with the class, discuss these changes and add your own ideas.

- Extended appointment hours to see a psychotherapist; some have walk-in service.
- 100% medical insurance coverage for off-campus services.
- Creation of education and outreach programs aimed at making students more comfortable in seeking help.
- Support groups for those coming out as gays and lesbians and for minority students.
- Your idea.

To learn more about mental illness, you can log on to a number of web sites. One you can begin with is the interactive web site "Ask PsychMD" at: www.askpsychmd.com/index.htm. To search for other sites, type in "mental illness" or a specific disorder such as bipolar disorder and find one that will give you the information you want. Here are a few suggestions:

- Sleep Disorders
- Childhood Depression
- Postpartum Depression – an illness a woman can get after giving birth
- Anxiety Disorder

AIDS *page 189 (CD 2 TRACK 27)*

Introduction

AIDS affects large numbers of people, not only in the United States, but all over the world. Three million people die of AIDS every year, and 40 million are infected, most of them in Africa. About 900,000 Americans are infected with the AIDS virus, and a quarter of them do not know it. AIDS is caused by a virus, called human immunodeficency virus (HIV). According to a recent report from the United Nations, the epidemic is still in its early stages, with HIV being transmitted in almost every part of the world.

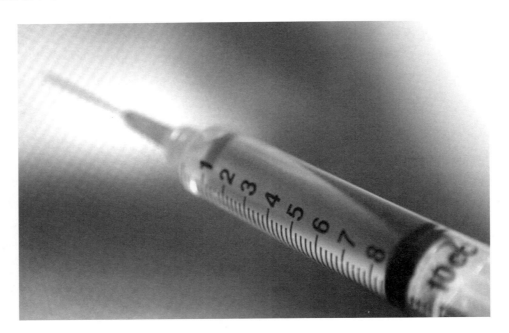

Dictogloss ❀

Listen to a complete sentence only once and write down the words you can remember. Then try to reconstruct the sentence. Finally, do the quiz.

1.

2

3.

4.

5.

Quiz

1. A person can become infected with HIV by
    A. drinking from the same cup as someone with HIV.
    B. hugging and touching someone with HIV.
    C. going swimming with someone with HIV.
    D. none of the above.

2. HIV is <u>not</u> present in
    A. sweat.
    B. blood.
    C. semen and vaginal secretions.
    D. breast milk.

3. Spread of HIV by sexual transmission can be prevented by
    A. abstinence.
    B. practicing mutual monogamy with an uninfected partner.
    C. correct use of latex condoms.
    D. all of the above.

4. If you were infected with HIV, you might show symptoms
    A. within a few weeks.
    B. within a year.
    C. in 10 or more years.
    D. any of the above.

Dictation ❀ *Write the correct word or number in the blank space. Correct and discuss the dictation.*

_____ _____ ____ _____ _____ _____ in simple terms: _____

equals_____. It's a little different with HIV, since the virus can cause slow, subtle damage to

the immune system _____ _____ ____ _____ _____ _____ _____ ____.

Most health care providers use the term "HIV disease " to identify the variety of changes _____

_____ _____ _____ from initial infection to more advanced stages of

serious life-threatening illness.

_____ _____ _____ _____ _____ _____ _____, and a

quarter of them do not know it, _____ _____ the CDC (US Centers for Disease Control

and Prevention). _____ _____ are not getting any kind of care for their disease. More than _____ _____ are going _____ for HIV, and _____ _____

_____ _____ _____ through _____ _____ or _____

_____.

    Recent _____ suggests that _____ _____ _____ are living with

HIV or AIDS _____ _____ _____ _____. There is an estimated total _____

_____ _____ _____ _____ currently living in the US with HIV

infection. _____, _____ _____ _____ die of AIDS every year

and_____ _____ _____ _____, most of them in Africa.

    Recently Secretary of State Colin Powell, on an international MTV "town hall" show that reaches

_____ million homes in _____ countries, said that while he respected the views

of the church, "In my own judgment, _____ _____ _____ _____ to

prevent infection, and, _____, I not only support their use, I encourage their use among

young people who are sexually active and need to protect themselves."

    In countries that _____ _____ _____ _____ and made greater use of

condoms, the disease has been kept _____ _____. In Brazil a UN AIDS report in 2000

indicated that _____ _____ _____ aged _____ to _____ with casual sex partners

were using condoms with them, a much higher rate than in AIDS-affected countries. This, combined

with a drug treatment program _____ _____ _____ for HIV, has caused

Brazil's infection rate _____ _____.

Discussion ❀ *Discuss these questions with a partner. Share your ideas with the class.*

1. ____ Is there a serious AIDS problem in your country? If not, why not?

2. ____ Where did you learn about AIDS? Are there education programs in your elementary
   schools, high schools, and/or universities?

3. ____ What happens to people with AIDS in your country? Are there AIDS treatment programs?

4. ____ In the United States one of the ways drug addicts get AIDS is by sharing needles. Would
   you support a government program to distribute clean needles to drug addicts?

The Immaculate Americans *page 190 (CD 2 TRACK 28)*

Introduction

The human body has its natural odors, many of which are tolerated in different societies. But most Americans have no tolerance for any type of body odor. When an American says, "he has BO," there is an assumption that that person doesn't bathe regularly and doesn't use a deodorant. In the dictation, sociologist Jack Levin of Northeastern University, looks at "Immaculate Americans" and offers his view.

Dictation   ❀   *Write the correct word or number in the blank space. Correct and discuss the dictation.*

Body odor is _____ _____. Every year, we immaculate Americans spend more

money on _____ and _____ than we contribute to the United Way charity. In

addition, we probably pass more time _____, _____, spraying, bathing,

_____, and _____ than any other people in the history of the world. Every

American, in fact, learns from _____ _____ _____ that cleanliness is next to Godliness

– a sign that an individual is _____ _____ and _____. No wonder that

Americans spend more than _____ _____ _____ _____

_____ _____ — it's part of our culture.

In other parts of the world, however, we _____ _____ _____ neurotically

concerned with our _____ _____. In Europe, for example, Americans are

_____ _____ by their demands for a room with a _____ _____.

Meanwhile, their European _____ usually stay in _____ _____

_____, where they wash up daily in a small sink and take their _____

_____ _____ down the hall. In their own countries, anyone caught _____

twice a day would probably _____ _____ _____ either eccentric or ill.

Americans can hardly take credit (_____ _____), however, for inventing a concern

for cleanliness. Sniffing and _____ _____ have long been practiced by Eskimos,

Philippine Islanders, and Samoans, who _____ _____ _____ for a

pleasant odor. And bathing for purification is _____ _____ _____ practiced by

the early Hebrews, Muslims, and Hindus.

Discussion ❀ *Discuss these questions with a partner. Share your ideas with the class.*

1. _____ In the first paragraph, Levin says that Americans spend more money on staying clean than what they contribute to the United Way. What is the United Way?

2. _____ Showering twice a day may seem unnecessary. Why do you think some Americans feel the need to shower that often?

3. _____ Think of all the soap and soap-related products you can buy today. This would include anything to do with body cleanliness. Write down as many as you can think of. Compare your answers with those of your classmates. Which group came up with the longest list?

Discussion 2 ❀

Here are some common idioms with words like clean, smell, *and* stink *that Americans use. Can you guess what they mean?*

> She came out smelling like a rose.
> I smell a rat. *Or –* The detective smelled foul play.
> The whole situation stinks.
> He leads a clean life. *Or –* He's a clean-cut type of guy.
> The bride made a clean break with tradition.
> The boxer is a clean fighter.
> The police tried to get the suspect to "come clean."
> The robber made a clean getaway from the bank.
> The bullet passed clean through the man's stomach.
> That last bet at the blackjack table cleaned me out.
> She cleaned out her car.
> The kids cleaned up their room.
> She cleaned up at the blackjack table.
> It's time to clear the air and tell the truth about this disgraceful situation.
> At summer camp we had lots of good, clean fun.

Plastics Alert *page 191 (CD 2 TRACK 29)*

Introduction

We all know that there are certain chemicals in our environment that are harmful to us. One of those toxic carcinogens is called dioxin. Dr. Edward Fujimoto, manager of a wellness program at a hospital, tells us about dioxins and how bad they are for us. In the movie "Erin Brockovich," companies secretly dumped dioxin into waterways, causing serious health problems in surrounding communities.

Paragraph Dictogloss ❀

Listen to the paragraph twice. You can listen without taking notes or take notes as you listen. Do not try to write every word. After you have finished listening, write one sentence (of at least 12-15 words) that is the main idea of the message. When you are finished, your teacher will give you the paragraph again. Come to agreement with your class about the main idea of the article.

Here are a few words with their abbreviations to help: microwave (mw),   release (rls),   ceramic (cer),   dioxin (dx),   heat (ht),   cells (cls)

Discussion ❀ *Discuss these questions with a partner. Share your ideas with the class.*

1. ____   If you buy TV dinners, soups, and other foods that come in plastic containers, what two steps should you follow before using your microwave?

2. ____   Americans buy billions of white coffee filters, paper towels, and paper napkins. They are white because they are bleached. The process of bleaching paper is responsible for creating dioxin. What alternatives are there for using these paper products?

3. ____   To make plastic wrap cling, manufacturers add "plasticizers," potentially harmful chemicals that can work their way into your food. This can be even more serious if you use it in a microwave. What alternatives are there for storing leftover food or heating food without this wrap?

4. ____   What other harmful chemicals can you find in your apartment or home? Make a list and compare your answers with the class.

Stem Cell Research *page 192 (CD 2 TRACK 30)*

Introduction

Genetic research has resulted in, and is resulting in, some of the most important medical break-throughs in many years. On the other hand, it has also resulted in great controversies about serious ethical questions.

Dictation ❀ *Write the correct word or number in the blank space. Correct and discuss the dictation.*

In therapeutic cloning, _____ _____ _____ _____, genetic material from a patient _____ _____ _____ a hollowed-out egg, and then artificially stimulated to grow, creating an embryo genetically identical to the patient. _____ _____ _____ _____ _____ _____ from these week-old embryos, then mold the flexible cells into easily used replacement tissue for patients. _____ _____ _____ _____ ____ _____, ethically troubling many.

Scientists overwhelmingly oppose implanting cloned embryos in women _____ _____ _____, _____ _____ _____. Several maverick researchers claim to have implanted women, _____ ____ _____ _____. However, many mainstream scientists worry that such attempts could proliferate _____ _____ _____ _____ and researchers become more proficient.

Discussion ❀ *Discuss these questions with a partner. Share your ideas with the class.*

1. _____ These are some of the positions that people have taken on stem cell research and cloning.

     a. There should be no stem cell research. We should not interfere with the work of God.

     b. Stem cell research is possible as long as we use "adult stem cells" only, because we should not kill embryonic cells. (Adult stem cells may not be as effective.)

     c. For the purpose of curing terrible human disease, we should be able to clone human embryos and take their cell stems, which can be used to grow new organs and tissues for disease research. However, we oppose reproductive cloning.

     d. We believe that everything is acceptable and inevitable, including reproductive cloning.

What is your opinion? Please talk about the advantages and disadvantages of your position.

2. _____ Isaac Asimov, in an essay titled, "There's No Way to Go but Ahead," said, "A double-edged sword of good and evil has hung over human technology from the beginning. The invention of knives and spears increased man's food supply and improved the art of murder. The discovery of nuclear energy now places all the earth under threat of destruction — yet it also offers the possibility of fusion power as an alternative energy source."

Will this quotation be true for stem cell research? What are some of the good and bad things that may occur as a result of this new medical technology?

Dictation ❀ *Listen to these two opinions and then state your own.*

Stacia Poulos has two cats, _____ _____ _____ _____. But she'd never want _____ _____ _____ _____ with either one of them.

"I'm not one for cloning. I'm not for it all," the 23-year-old Scituate resident said _____ _____ _____ _____ about researchers in Texas cloning a cat.

" It will lead _____ _____ _____ and that is wrong. _____ _____ _____ _____. Sheep, and now this step," she said, as she prepared to get on a train at the Quincy Adams MBTA station this morning.

She said _____ _____ _____, even if it means getting duplicates for Picky and Toledo, her two cats. "_____ _____ _____ _____ _____, but I wouldn't clone them."

Jim Hyland, 33, of Braintree said, "_____ _____ _____. Cats shouldn't be cloned. Nobody should be cloned. They're spending _____ _____ _____ _____, when they could be spending it on research for something useful: find a cure for AIDS or cancer." Hyland has a dog, a fox terrier named Max. "I love Max. He's 12 years old and I don't know what I would do if he died today. _____ _____ _____ _____ _____ _____, _____ _____. Unfortunately, _____ _____."

Discussion ❀ *Discuss these questions with a partner. Share your ideas with the class.*

If you had a cat or dog that you loved dearly and it was going to die soon, would you clone it if you had the opportunity? Why or why not?

Alternative Medicine *page 193 (CD 2 TRACK 31)*

Introduction

In 1976, when President Richard Nixon established diplomatic relations with the People's Republic of China, Americans learned about acupuncture, which the Chinese had been practicing for centuries. Since then and into the twenty-first century Americans have become increasingly interested in acupuncture and other forms of "alternative medicine."

Dictation ❀ *Write the correct word or number in the blank space. Correct and discuss the dictation.*

_____ _____ _____, the idea of treating pain with acupuncture or hypnosis would

have _____ _____ _____ _____ within the medical mainstream. _____

_____ _____ _____ _____ _____ _____ are offering patients

alternative or complementary therapies _____ _____ _____

_____.

A big reason for the trend _____ _____ _____. A 1997 Harvard study

reported _____ _____ _____ _____ _____ _____ to

alternative practitioners _____ _____ _____ _____ _____ to

primary care doctors, spending $27 billion (a good part of it _____ _____ _____)

on alternative treatments.

Proponents say complementary techniques, particularly mind-body therapies, _____

_____ _____. They are non-invasive and have _____ _____ _____.

And they tap into the healing power of the mind.

Discussion ❀ *Discuss these questions with a partner. Share your ideas with the class.*

1. ____ Are alternative medicine practices popular in your country?

2. ____ Have you, or anyone in your family, ever gone to an acupuncturist?

3. ____ Which do you have more faith in – Eastern medicine or Western medicine?

Dictation ❀

After doing the dictation, match these complementary techniques to the description.

       A. Hypnosis   B. Relaxation Therapy   C. Massage Therapy

                  D. Acupuncture   E. Biofeedback

(_____) 1. Complementary care uses variations of touch, _____ _____ _____ to deep

tissue manipulation. The most common technique is _____ _____, in which

the muscles are stroked or kneaded _____ _____ _____ _____

_____.

(_____) 2. A mind-body technique in which the patient _____ _____ _____; in this

state the _____ _____ _____ _____ _____ to ease symptoms of pain.

(_____) 3. _____ _____ this ancient Chinese technique, _____ _____ _____

_____ _____ _____ called Qi (pronounced chee) which travels through

channels in the body. Pain or illness results when channels become blocked. To restore

flow, _____ _____ _____ _____ at specific points on the _____ _____,

(_____) 4. Complementary techniques include guided imagery, a form of self-hypnosis in which the

patient visualizes positive images _____ _____ _____; progressive muscle

relaxation, in which the patient tenses, _____, and then _____ muscle

groups; and _____, in which the patient _____ ____ _____ _____

_____ by focusing on a _____ _____ _____.

(_____) 5. A mind-body technique that uses sensors to measure physiological functions like muscle

tension or gastrointestinal activity; _____ _____ _____ the "feedback"

on a monitor, _____ _____ _____ of how their bodies respond and learn

how to control that response.

Discussion ❀ *Discuss these questions with a partner. Share your ideas with the class.*

1. _____ Do you believe that there is a strong mind-body connection and that these therapies can help someone who is sick and in pain?

2 _____ Do you think that medical insurance should pay for these therapies?

A Smoking Issue *page 194 (CD 2 TRACK 32)*

Introduction

Since the 1970s more and more public and private places in the US have become smoke-free. In many areas cigarette smokers must put on heavy clothing in wintry weather and smoke their much-needed cigarette outdoors because it is the only place left where a smoker can smoke.

Dictation   ❀   *Write the correct word or number in the blank space. Correct and discuss the dictation.*

College campuses are the latest battleground for _____ and _____ – _____. Since _____ _____ _____ _____ _____, cities and towns throughout the nation have forced restaurants and bars_____ _____ _____ – _____. In step with the times, colleges _____ _____ _____ have gone smoke-free or are considering the move. Recently, Smith College _____ _____ _____ _____ _____ and the University of Connecticut _____ _____.

A 1999 study by the Harvard School of Public Health found that _____ of non-commuter colleges and universities banned smoking everywhere — including _____ _____ _____ – while _____ allowed it in residence halls.

For smokers' rights activists, the move _____ _____ _____ _____ _____ _____ is _____ _____ _____ in an anti-American drive to _____ _____ and control a _____ _____ _____ _____. Barbara Aucoin, president of the Massachusetts chapter of Fight Ordinances and Restrictions to Control and Eliminate Smoking (FORCES), is _____ _____ smoking bans in college housing. She refers to _____ _____ _____ of local health boards to ban smoking in bars and restaurants as "Nazi tactics."

"The _____ to ban smoking _____ _____ _____ _____ the individual owners rather than the government," she said. "You take away that choice and we are not Americans anymore."

Kevin Kroner, Executive Director of Northeastern University's Tobacco Control Resource Center, said, "Your right to put these substances into your body should _____ _____ _____ _____ your neighbor's lungs."

A research group for student affairs and institutional research conducted a survey of _____ _____ _____. ____ _____ ____ _____ _____, smokers and non-smokers, said that smoking in private rooms ____ _____ _____within some halls is the preferred policy.

Discussion ❊ *Discuss these questions with a partner. Share your ideas with the class.*

1. _____ Do you smoke? Have you ever smoked?

2. _____ Are there areas in your country where smoking is not allowed?

3. _____ People eat food that is bad for their arteries and heart. Yet eating this kind of food is not forbidden. Why don't we ban this food as well?

4. _____ In the article, Aucoin said, "the anti-smoking movement could be just the beginning of a steady dwindling of basic freedoms." Do you think this is true?

Discussion ❊

Look at the following graphs. With a partner, discuss the questions that follow the graphs.

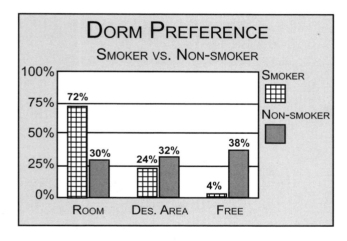 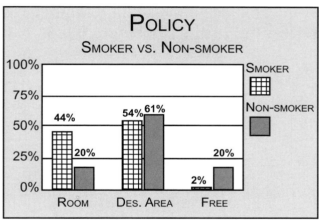

1. _____ How many smokers believe smokers should be allowed to smoke in their rooms?

2. _____ How many non-smokers believe that smokers should be allowed to smoke in their rooms?

3. _____ How many smokers believe that there should be a policy forbidding smokers to smoke in their rooms?

4._____ How many non-smokers believe that there should be a policy forbidding smokers to smoke in their rooms?

5. _____ What other information do you learn from these graphs?

6. _____ What conclusions can you make from this information?

Dictation: Judge for Yourself   ❀ *Write the word in the blank space. Correct the dictation.*

Vinny lived in an apartment _____ _____ _____ _____ that of a woman who

was a cigarette smoker. He filed a nuisance suit against her, claiming _____ _____ _____

_____ _____ through vents and cracks _____ _____ _____ _____ _____.

The woman did not believe _____ _____ _____ _____ _____ _____was

an illegal activity. She told the judge _____ _____ _____ _____ _____ _____

_____ did not qualify as a nuisance and cited the fact that there was no mention of _____

_____ _____ _____ _____ _____.

Discussion   ❀ *Discuss these questions with a partner. Share your ideas with the class.*

1. _____ Have you ever been bothered by second-hand smoke?
2. _____ If you go to a hotel, do you ask for a non-smoking room?
3. _____ Do you think that the judge ruled "for" or "against" Vinny?

The Verdict ❀

The judge _____ _____ Vinny, ruling that the smoke _____ _____ _____

_____ _____ _____ was _____ _____ _____ _____

_____.

Full Dictation Texts

Immigration Statistics *page 1 (CD 1 TRACK 1)*

❀ Dictation

1. Since the founding of the U.S., more than **55 million immigrants** from every **continent** have settled here.

2. **During the 1990s** an average of more than **one million** immigrants, legal and **illegal**, settled in the U.S. each year.

3. Legal immigration **fluctuates** between **700,000** and **900,000** each year, and the INS estimates that **420,000 illegal aliens** settle here each year.

4. **Since 1970** more than **26 million** immigrants have settled here, representing about **one-third** of all people **ever to come**.

5. The largest number of legal immigrants to come in the **70s** and **80s** came from **Vietnam**, Cambodia, Laos, Mexico, El Salvador, Guatemala, and Haiti.

6. Of the immigrant groups, there are **30 million** Latinos, now the **largest** minority, **outnumbering African-Americans**.

7. In California, home to over **4 million** Asian-Americans, **75%** of all Californians are working for **Asian-owned** businesses or paying rent to an Asian **landlord**.

Men Putting Family First _page 2 (cd 1 track 2)_

❈ Dictation

While previous studies **portrayed** American men as more **concerned about** power, prestige, or money than about their families, **new findings** from The Radcliffe Public Policy Center indicate men between the ages of **20 and 39** are more likely to **put family matters first**.

In releasing its **national survey** of attitudes about work, life, and family relationships, Radcliffe said the findings suggest a **generational shift**, with younger men **breaking ranks** with their fathers and grandfathers.

The study involved phone interviews with **482** men and **526** women. The **margin of error** is plus or minus **5** percentage points.

Of the male participants between ages twenty and **39**, about **82** % placed time with family at the top of a wish list that included **flexible schedules**. Additionally, **71** % said they would give up a portion of their pay **to ensure** they could have more time with their families. In contrast, **80** % of the men between **40** and **49** said doing work that allowed them to **utilize their skills** was more important than community service, additional family time, or **job security**. Of men **50 to 64, 82** % said they were chiefly concerned with developing good relations **with coworkers**.

"The men who are in their **60s** have always seen themselves as **sole breadwinners**," said Paula Rayman, director of the Radcliffe Center. "If you look at the **research conducted** over the years, you'll find that the **baby boomers** in their **40s and 50s** grew up thinking of themselves as **primary breadwinners**. Younger men, however, are working **alongside women**, and they are more likely to talk about sharing family responsibilities and **about equality**."

When Harris **pollsters** interviewed women ages **20 to 39**, they pinpointed **another trend: 25** % said they did not plan to have any children, up from **19** % in a **1993** survey. "These are young women with **dual income parents** or people with single parents who now feel that it's impossible **to do it all**," Rayman said. These young women are not saying they are not going to get married, but they are **ambivalent about** having children. And what we are seeing is that the average age for women to have children **has increased from 21** years old to approximately **27** years old, a **five-year jump** for the first child.

Staying in the Nest *page 4 (CD 1 TRACK 3)*

❦ Dictation

The caps and gowns have been used and returned, yet many Baby Boomers are finding **that the commencement** to their grown-up kids' life away from home has been **put off** indefinitely.

In a development that **would have repulsed** many boomers in the generation-gap days of **their own youth**, returning to the nest – or **not leaving** it – is becoming increasingly commonplace. A **weaker economy** and **shrinking job market** appear to have accelerated the trend and produced more of what American Demographics magazine calls "**boomerangers**."

This year, about **670,000** or **56** % of university graduates plan to live **with their parents** for some period of time. Sociologists and other observers say that besides the **financial reasons**, boomers themselves – those turning **37** to **55** this year – are **encouraging the trend**.

"The negative thing about moving home has really **been reversed,**" says author Faith Popcorn. "A lot of parents have a **best-friend relationship** with their kids. I think **baby boomer** parents really have gotten the idea that home is **fun and casual,** and they never wanted their kids to leave **in the first place**.

The financial security of the most **prosperous generation ever** and their bigger houses have made this **once-unthinkable** living arrangement much more appealing **to both sides**. Ward Simpson and his wife have two sons and a daughter **who keep going away** and coming back, going away and moving back. "**Most parents complain** that their children never visit them but mine never leave – and I **have no problem with that**."

The **moving back** trend first emerged in the 1980s before **flattening out** in the 1990s. Now it is on the increase again following the **dot-com crash** and with the first **wave** of Baby Boomers' **71** million children **reaching adulthood**.

The trend **may fade** when boom times return, but it looks **unlikely to go away** The U.S. Census shows **18** million Americans ages **18** to **34** live with their parents – a group now **drawing attention** from marketers because it has lots of disposable income and **is growing steadily**.

Marriage and Divorce *page 6 (CD 1 TRACK 4)*

❧ Dictation

1. People with a college degree **tend to marry later** and stay married.

2. Among married women ages 25 to **44** with a college degree, 15 **out of 1000** divorced within a year, compared with **30** out of 1000 women with just a **high school diploma**.

3. People's average age at their first marriage **increased** to **24.9** years for women and **27.1** for men.

4. In the 1950s and 1960s the **average age** for women to marry was **20** and for men it was **24**.

5. Divorce is least likely to **occur** among **Asians** and most likely to occur among **African-Americans**.

❧ Dictogloss

1. About 9 out of 10 Americans are expected to marry at least once in their lifetime.

2. Half of first marriages end in divorce but 3 in 4 will probably remarry.

3. First marriages that end in divorce typically last about 8 years.

4. The earlier people are married, the more likely they are to get divorced.

5. Among younger men, having an older wife is becoming more common.

❧ Dictation

My parents are **divorced**. I live with my mother. I spend two **weekends** a month with my dad and one month in the summer with him. I love my father but he has **remarried**, and I don't really like his new wife, Amy. My father is real nice to me and takes me places, but Amy **sort of resents me** and I feel uncomfortable around her.

Now that I'm 15, I **would rather** spend more time at home with my friends. I also want to get a **part-time** job this summer. Do you think my father will be **hurt** if I don't visit him this summer? What do you think I should do?

Open Adoption *page 8 (CD 1 TRACK 5)*

❀ Dictation

Q. Why did you choose an open adoption?

A. This is a big question, but it **boils down to this**; once we got over the fear that everyone seems to have at first, we **recognized the benefits** of openness. Without the secrecy involved in traditional, **closed type** adoption, there will never be the questions of: "Why did my birthmom **place me here**?" Or, "I wonder **whatever happened** to my baby?" Or, "**Is my baby happy**?" or "What kind of woman **gave birth** to this child?" When there are answers **instead of mysteries**, it's better and healthier for everyone.

Q. Aren't you worried that the birthmom will want her baby back?

A. **One of the benefits** of the agency we went with, is the excellent counseling that was provided to both us and our children's birthmoms. **As a result** of this counseling, we were all comfortable with our **situations and decisions**. Because of this comfort, **there was less fear** of a reclaim situation. Also, we knew that the agency we used followed the **legal process** and provided for a fairly secure relinquishment of **birthparents' parental rights**. This was the only way we **would have considered** doing our second adoption.

Q. Are you going to maintain contact with your sons' birthmoms?

A. Yes, we have a very **special relationship** with our sons' birthmoms. We live **fairly close** to Will's birthmom and visit **frequently**. We have been to Will's **half-sister's** birthday party, and they came to Will's first birthday party. We **often exchange** email and cards. Our sons will always have their **birthmoms** in **their lives**, as well as another set of **grandparents**!

(There's **no such thing** as too many Grandmas and Grandpas!) Many people seem to think that **having birthparents** involved would **be like co-parenting** or maybe a step-parent relationship. This **is not the case.** We are the "**real** and **forever**" parents of our children.

Note to teachers:

In an open adoption, the amount of time that children are in contact with their birthparents varies quite a bit. In some cases, the birthmother is in contact only once a year because she lives out of state or has married and moved on to start her own family.

In an open adoption, adoptive parents can make initial rejections. For example, if the adoptive baby has parents on drugs, or parents with a history of mental illness or physical or mental abuse, they can tell the agency that they are not interested in that particular baby without any repercussions.

Open adoption agencies can charge between $10,000 and $20,000 for their services. Some of the money goes to the medical fees of the birthmother.

Older children and children with special needs such as mental retardation or those in the Deering family are usually available "free of charge." The state determines when they are legally free for adoption. These children are not part of the open adoption system but are part of a state agency that oversees their welfare.

You may also want to mention that more and more Americans are going abroad to adopt. Discuss the reasons why there are fewer and fewer American children to adopt (because of birth control/abortion and the fact that many girls opt to keep their babies now that it is no longer a scandal).

For more information, students can visit the following web sites:

OpenAdopt.com
or **Host33.com/scfl/**
or **e-mail:scfl@host33.com**

Three Little Words *page 10 (CD 1 TRACK 6)*

❧ Dictation

When you think about it, we've all raised our kids using a minimum of three exclamatory sentences: **No! Don't**! and **Stop**! Used unsparingly, they can take a parent through **20** or **30** years of living. **No television** until **you've done** your homework. No dessert until **you've cleaned up** your plate. No hurry because you're not going. **No way**. No **dishes, no** movie. No time for your **mother**? No more **arguing with your brother**. No! And **that's** the last time I say it.

Just when you think there are no more ways to say "No," along comes "Don't." Don't **screw up**. Don't forget your **sweater**. Don't **do as I** do, do as I say. Don't **forget** to say **thank you**. Don't you hear **what I'm saying**? Don't make me **say** it again.

For sheer drama, there is nothing like "Stop!" Stop **humming**. Stop **driving me crazy**. Stop dating **that creep**. Stop acting like **you're a big shot**. Stop **trying** to be something you're not. Stop **being so negative.**

They're all familiar. We **couldn't have survived** without them. But wouldn't it be **sad** if No! Don't! and Stop! were the only things they learned from us ... and those three little words shaped their lives.

Sexual Orientation: Questions and Answers

page 12 (CD 1 TRACK 7)

❧ Dictation

1. What is sexual orientation?

Sexual orientation is an emotional, **romantic**, sexual, or affectational attraction to another person. It includes heterosexuality, homosexuality, and various forms of **bisexuality**. Most scientists today agree that **sexual orientation** is most likely the result of a complex interaction of **biological**, cognitive, and environmental factors. In most people, sexual orientation is shaped **at an early age**.

2. Is sexual orientation a choice?

    No. Human beings cannot choose to be either **gay** or **straight**. Mental health professionals do not consider sexual orientation to be a **conscious choice**. There is considerable evidence to suggest that biology, including **genetic** or **inborn** hormonal factors, plays a significant role in a person's sexuality.

3. Can therapy change sexual orientation?

    No. Even though most homosexuals live **successful, happy** lives, some homosexual or bisexual people may seek to change their sexual orientation through therapy because they are often **pressured** by family members or religious groups to try and do so. **The reality is** that homosexuality is not an illness. It does not require treatment and **is not changeable**.

4. Is homosexuality a mental disorder or emotional problem?

    No. Psychologists and other **mental health** professionals agree that it is not an illness, mental **disorder**, or emotional problem. **This belief** is based on 35 years of objective, well-designed research.

5. Why is it important for society to be better educated about homosexuality?

    Educating all people about sexual orientation and homosexuality is likely to diminish **anti-gay prejudice**. Accurate information is especially important to young people who are first discovering and **seeking** to **understand** their sexuality – whether homosexual, bisexual, or heterosexual.

6. Is there any legislation against anti-gay violence?

    Yes. Some states include violence **against an individual** on the basis of his or her sexual orientation as a "**hate-crime**," and ten U.S. states have laws against discrimination **on the basis of** sexual orientation.

Older Learners *page 14 (CD 1 TRACK 8)*

❀ Pair Dictation

Did anyone predict there would be so many adult students? Nobody in 1980 assumed that the number of adults going to college would be so high today. Of the 15 million students in college, almost half of them are adults with kids and jobs. The Joe College stereotype – the 18 to 22-year-old full-time student in residence on campus – accounts for only 20 percent of the 15 million students.

❀ Dictation

For Chi-Hing Wong, **nothing is more important** than **education**. That's why at age **68** she decided to go back to school to **get her high school diploma**. Next week Wong will don a cap and gown and receive a Boston Public Schools diploma in **ceremonies** at Faneuil Hall **on the eve of the Chinese New Year**.

"It has always been my dream to go back to school," said Wong, **who will be 69 in two weeks** and plans to attend college. "**No matter what age you are**, you can learn. It is never too late."

Wong moved to Boston from China in **1975**. **While she had been** a teacher in China and Okinawa, she did not speak English, **nor did she have the credentials** to teach here. So she went to work in a day care center and concentrated on **taking care of her family**. She also took adult education classes and English classes. When a broken hip forced her to retire **from her day care job in 1992**, Wong saw an opportunity. **Her children were grown**, and she had plenty of free time, but she worried **that she was too old to go back to school**.

While visiting her daughter and son-in-law in California, she met a college professor who encouraged her **to further her education**. "He could speak **nine** languages," Wong recalled. "I told him I wanted to learn, but I was too old. He encouraged me; **he told me I could do it**."

❀ Dictation 2: Judge for Yourself

A man **attending** a small university **had started** his **graduate** course of study **17** years earlier. At that time he **had moved** into student housing and **had been** living there ever since. The university tried to **evict** the man because he only took an **occasional** course and never **completed** the **requirements** for a degree. The man **claimed** he was a student and could not be **forced** to leave. The university took the matter to court.

❀ The Verdict

The court ruled **against** the student and held that it was **the school's right** to decide **who was a student**. The man **should move out** and **let** someone **more serious** about **earning** a **degree occupy** the room.

The Psychology of Shopping *page 17 (CD 1 TRACK 9)*

❀ Dictation 1

1. **Market** research **has** found that the color **light purple makes** customers feel like spending money. TRUE

2. Upon entering a store, most **shoppers** head **straight** ahead. FALSE (they go to the right)

3. The only **reason** that people shop is that they **need** something. FALSE (there are many reasons)

4. The **main** reason that people shop on the **internet** is that there is no **sales pressure**. FALSE (most people said it was easy to place an order)

5. Women **have a greater** affinity for shopping **than** men. TRUE

6. **Closed-circuit** surveillance TVs are **illegal** in stores. FALSE (most large stores use them to prevent shoplifting)

7. **Express lanes** were **introduced** to reduce shopper **frustration**. TRUE

❀ Dictation 2

1. The use of shopping as a **social activity** seems **unchanged**, however. Women like to shop with friends **egging** each other on, and **rescuing** each other from ill-advised **purchases**. I don't think **we'll** see two men **set off** on a day of **hunting** for the **perfect** bathing suit. As **we've seen, studies** show that when two women shop together, they **often** spend more time and money than women alone. They certainly can **outshop** and **outspend** women saddled with **male** companions.

2. Here's an example. The **trademark** of The Gap and many other clothing stores is that you can easily **touch, stroke, unfold** and otherwise examine at **close range** everything on the selling floor. A lot of **sweaters** and **shirts** are sold thanks to the decision to foster **intimate** contact between **shopper** and **goods**.

❀ Dictation 3 and Decision Making

1. You buy a scarf from a discount store as a gift for a friend who is very **label** conscious. You have an empty box from a **trendy** store. Do you repackage the scarf in the box and give it to your friend?

2. A good friend has **just bought** a very **expensive** sweater and **asked** you if you like it. You think it is **awful**. Do you say so?

3. You're in an **exclusive** boutique. While trying on **clothes** in the **dressing room**, you get **lipstick** on a **designer** dress. Do you inform the salesperson?

4. You **accidentally** drop your new amplifier and it no longer works. There is no **visible** evidence of the accident. Do you try to return it without mentioning the **accident**?

5. The **price tag** on the suit you are buying is $280 but the salesperson **has** only **rung up** $28. Do you ask if there is a **mistake**?

Television *page 19 (CD 1 TRACK 10)*

❀ Pair Dictation

1. In 1980 only 10% of American homes had a television, but by 1990 the percentage had grown to 90%. FALSE (in <u>1950</u> only 10% of American homes had televisions)

2. The average American child will witness over 200,000 acts of violence on television, including 16,000 murders before age 18. TRUE

3. Watching TV has been linked to obesity in children. TRUE

4. Children mostly watch TV with friends or family. FALSE (a large percentage of them watch it alone)

5. Ninety-five percent of homes have a television. In fact, more families own a television than a phone. TRUE

6. The average child spends approximately 56 hours a week watching television. FALSE (28 hours a week)

7. Forty-six percent of all television violence identified by a study took place in children's cartoons. TRUE

8. Studies show that higher rates of television viewing are correlated with increased tobacco usage, increased alcohol intake, and younger onset of sexual activity.   TRUE

❀ Dictation 2

Most of us **are at least** **dimly aware** of the addictive power of television **through our own experiences** with the medium: **our compulsive involvement with the tube** too often keeps us **from talking to each other**, from **working and learning**, and from getting involved in community affairs. And yet, **we cannot seem to turn the set off**, or even not turn it on in the first place. **Doesn't this sound like an addiction?**

❀ Dictation 3: Judge for Yourself

Jerry, **a fifteen-year-old boy living in Florida**, broke into his neighbor's house, shot the **eighty-year-old** woman, and escaped in her car. At the trial, **the defense pleaded not guilty** to the charges by reason of temporary insanity brought on by Jerry **watching too much television**. He watched **more than six hours a day, loved crime shows,** and had just watched a movie which contained scenes similar to **the murder he had committed.**

❀ The Verdict

The court ruled **AGAINST** Jerry, stating that there was **no evidence** that **television destroyed** the ability to distinguish **right from wrong**.

Movies *page 22 (CD 1 TRACK 11)*

❀ Dictation

Toula is **30**. And **unmarried**. Which means as a nice Greek girl she's a **failure**. All her **cousins** did the right thing – married Greek boys and made Greek babies. So everyone **worries** – what will **become of** Toula?

Then one day she sees the **ultimate** unattainable guy and realizes the only way her life will get better is if she **gets away** from her big, fat Greek family. Toula escapes from the family restaurant. She **exchanges** her seating hostess jacket for a **college diploma**, convinces her aunt to give her a new job, and **trades in** her coke-bottle glasses for contact lenses, **just in time** for "him" to walk back into her life.

Ian Miller is tall, handsome, but definitely not Greek. Their **courtship** is an Olympian **culture clash**. Can Ian handle Toula, her parents, her aunt, uncles, cousins, and several **centuries** of **Greek heritage**? Will Toula discover the love she's been missing right **in the heart** of her big, fat family?

One thing is **for sure**: for **better** or for **worse**, for richer or for **poorer**, with Ian's proposal, Toula is **headed** for her big, fat Greek wedding.

Cults on Campus *page 24 (CD 1 TRACK 12)*

❀ Dictation

Shawn, student at UCLA:

In the middle of my freshman year, I was having a **tough time socially**, since I broke up with my girlfriend and my roommate **was always out with** friends. So when this friendly-looking guy came up to me on campus he **caught me** when I was **in a real funk**. He was very nice and polite, and we talked about **campus issues** and friends. After a while he asked me to think about coming and **joining a group** he was in where I could make some **new connections.** I decided to **give it a shot**. But when I was at the second long "meeting" I began to feel I was getting **sucked into** something I wasn't sure about . . . like they started making me **feel guilty and ashamed** about everything I did. Then they made some remarks about how I'd **be better off** limiting contact with family and friends. Even though I was feeling **depressed**, it didn't feel right. I felt a **tremendous relief** when I decided not to go back.

Karen, student at NYU:

When I arrived here, I was really excited **about coming** to a new city to study. It was my first time away from home and I was psyched to **break away from** my old life and meet new friends. One day in the cafeteria, a **nice-looking guy,** who I thought was a student, **approached me** and we got talking. At first it was about family and friends, and we really seemed to **hit it off,** but later on into the conversation, I **figured out** that he wasn't a student here. Then he started **making suggestions** that I come to his church club where I could make new friends. After a half hour I was getting **really bad vibes** about the way he tried to **latch on** to me. Finally, I told him to **get lost**. When I wrote about this in my journal to my English professor, she told me that there are about 3,000 cults **operating in** the U.S., and that the **fast-growing** cult, the International Churches of Christ, **has been banned** from at least **39 colleges**.

Note to teachers:

New recruits to an organization are often brought to meetings before they realize that it is not school-sanctioned. By that time, they have made connections with group members, and it's difficult to leave. The emotional strain can be intense, especially if the recruit feels as though there's nowhere else to turn.

page 26 (CD 1 TRACK 13)

Are You Superstitious?

❈ Dictation

A superstition is an **illogical belief** that some action will affect something else **that is unrelated to the action**. Many people believe, **for example**, that breaking a mirror will result in **seven years of bad luck**. When one speaks of good fortune, **knocking on wood** is said to ensure its continuation. **Lucky charms**, rabbits' feet, and other amulets provide insurance to keep the possessor safe.

Many superstitions began **in religious belief**. The cat has been worshipped by several cultures, including the ancient Egyptian. The fear **that a black cat** crossing one's path will bring misfortune may come from the old belief **in its power**.

Many athletes have their own superstitious **rituals**. They often make a connection **between a victory** and some article of clothing or jewelry. **When questioned about this,** most will reply **that they don't want to take chances**.

Belief in certain superstitions **tends to run in families**. Most people **who throw spilled salt over their shoulders** saw their parents doing the same thing **when they were young**. They may, **or may not**, know that the original reason was to keep the devil **from getting too close**.

One danger of superstition is that it encourages people to believe that their future is **out of their hands**. However, most of us who **knock on wood**, carry a lucky charm when we fly, and never walk **under a ladder** say that our behavior is due to habit or sentiment.

❀ **Pair Dictation**

A young Japanese woman named Keiko was being wheeled into operating room four when she noticed the number over the door. She began to cry softly. The nurse became concerned and asked what was wrong. Keiko was embarrassed, but explained that the Japanese character for the number four is pronounced the same as the character for the word "death." Already concerned about her health, Keiko was disturbed to be wheeled into a room labeled "death." Although she said it was just a silly superstition, Keiko was unable to let go of her fear.

The surgery went well despite the room number, but the patient suffered needless anxiety. Had the hospital personnel mentioned to Keiko that she was being scheduled for room four, her feelings might have become known in time to reschedule her surgery into a different room. Room number three, for example, would have been appropriate because "three" in Japanese characters also means "life."

Make a Difference! Be a Volunteer!
❀ **Dictation**
page 30 (CD 1 TRACK 14)

Like millions of other people, Perry Flicker saw the World Trade Center Towers <u>**collapse on TV**</u>. The world's towers, he thought. How could he <u>**sit by and watch**</u>? So when he heard <u>**volunteers**</u> were needed to deliver water, Gatorade, candy, and <u>**goggles**</u> to the disaster site, he raced the <u>**35 miles**</u> from his office in New Jersey to what became known as <u>**Ground Zero**</u>.

After that first <u>**exhausting**</u> and <u>**terrifying**</u> day in ash-covered ruins, he remained there. For two weeks, Flicker <u>**submerged himself**</u> in a personal need to help others, just as all Americans began a universal, <u>**marathon effort**</u> to shore up the <u>**human spirit**</u>.

"There were mounds of supplies <u>**on a dock**</u> there, so I couldn't leave," says Flicker, a <u>**hardware**</u> production supervisor for Intel Corp. in New Jersey. "I just started working on the <u>**pile**</u>. All night, sorting jeans, <u>**Power Bars**</u>, flashlights, gloves, sweatshirts, T-shirts. Then it just kept coming. I was up <u>**three and a half straight days**</u> without sleep."

Previously, Flicker was **hardly** a career volunteer. He had visited sick and lonely senior citizens. He had helped out with Salvation Army **drives**. Now, he'll never look at volunteers **the same way**.

"I **couldn't get over** the humility and compassion for people there," he says. "Firefighters were walking on **shards** and **twisted** metal to try to find **survivors**, and they were thanking me. Thanking me? **That's incredible**. Nobody felt like a hero there. We all just **felt like** people who had something to do."

❀ Dictation and Discussion

1. Josh Ryan, 48, of Bandera, Texas, invested $10,000,000 from his **pro basketball career** to open Ryan Ranch, a home to **1300** young adults, many of whom have been **abused or abandoned**.

2. Leon Goldberg, 68, of Detroit, Michigan, kept his **3000** workers on the **payroll** after a fire destroyed his **textile mill** last year. He **rebuilt** the plant, and all but **400** are now **back on the job**.

3. LaToya Jefferson, 51, of Milltown, Florida, is a **volunteer** at Paula's Place, a **homeless shelter** for African-American women. She has been there to cook for **five** hours a day for **ten** years and remains **friends** with the women, **even after they leave**.

4. Addie May Carlson, 75, of Oakdale, California, **has been running** low-cost summer camps for disabled children for five years. She accepts **no salary**.

5. Bob Dean, 36, of Chicago, Illinois, grew up in a poor **neighborhood** and knows what it's like to be on **probation**. One day he **showed up** at the courthouse and offered to help kids in **trouble**. He's been volunteering for **12** years, sometimes **30 hours** a week. "I've seen **a lot of pain**," he says.

6. Lena Chin, 52, of New York City, arrived from China in **1986** and soon began **volunteering** several days a week in her city's Chinatown to help Asian **immigrants** whose **inability** to speak and read English makes it impossible for them to fill out the **complicated** forms required for **health benefits**.

Winning in Las Vegas *page 32 (CD 1 TRACK 15)*

❀ Dictation

I need an unbiased person with a good **set of brains** to help me sort this out. A woman I work with (**we're compatible** friends) decided we should take our vacation together and go to Las Vegas and **gamble**, just **for the heck of it**. Nellie and I saved all year, and each of us was able to **save $1,800** for the trip. After travel and hotel expenses, we had just $**400 left** for gambling.

Nellie and I **had a terrific time**, saw some great shows, and **ate like royalty**. We lost some money at blackjack and the craps tables so we stopped and went for the **slot machines**, which we both love. We each had **$100** left, and decided to play the **one dollar** machines.

By 2:30 A.M., we were **tapped out**, and all the money we had **set aside** for gambling was gone. Nellie started to walk back to our rooms. I then said, "I'm going to put one last dollar in and **call it quits**." I stepped over to the slot that Nellie **had been feeding** all night, put in a dollar, and lo and behold, I **hit the jackpot**! The money was **falling** all over the floor, and it seemed like an **endless stream** of silver dollars was coming out. I **counted the total**, and it came to $1,200.

Nellie **yelled**, "You have to **split that with me**. I fed that machine all night!" I replied, "When you **walked away**, it became my machine. I **don't owe you** anything." She yelled, "What kind of a friend are you, **anyway**?" Well, I realized our friendship was **at stake**, and decided to **split my winnings** with Nellie. I would like to know, **was I a fool** to do it, or was I **morally obligated** to share my winnings? Please tell me what you think.

Tess in Texas

A Business That's "Going to the Dogs"

❀ Dictation

page 34 (CD 1 TRACK 16)

Reporter: Richard, how did you get into the **dog day care** business?

Richard: It all started when I agreed to **take care of** a neighbor's dog when she went on vacation for a week. She didn't want to put her dog **in a kennel** and since I have two dogs **of my own,** I said sure. Then when a friend had to take a **business trip** to Texas, he asked me to pet-sit his dogs. Then **word got around,** and more and more working people who worried about their dogs getting lonely during the day started calling me up. **One thing led to another** and here I am!

Reporter: So how many dogs do you have in your dog day care business now?

Richard: **It varies**; some days we have ten dogs, but we're licensed for **twelve**.

Reporter: Do all of the dogs come for day care while their owners are **at work**?

Richard: No, some come for **overnights or for a week or two** while the owners are on vacation. We have **comfy beds** and **doggie couches**.

Reporter: **That's cool**! What **kind of fees** do you charge?

Richard: If the owner **drops off** his dog, we charge $28.00 a day. If they want **round-trip pick up** in our van, the charge is higher, about 35 **bucks**.

Reporter: You provide transportation?

Richard: Yup. **Drivers** pick up the dogs beginning at 7:30 AM from their homes and drop them off at 5:00 PM. Dogs love **the ride**!

Reporter: Do you have any special **entrance requirements**?

Richard: Well, they have to be **housebroken,** of course. And they must have written proof of rabies and **other inoculations**. Once in a while there's a dog that doesn't **get along with** other dogs, but most love being here with their **buddies**.

Reporter: I can see that you love your job.

Richard: You've **gotta love dogs** to do this. And now that business **is booming,** I can hire more help!

Discussion/Guesses

79% give their pets Christmas or birthday presents

43% cook special food for their cats

33% talk to pets on the phone or answering machine

84% call themselves the animal's mother or father

21% sometimes dress up their pets for special occasions, such as Halloween

62% sign letters or cards from themselves and their pets

4% send their dogs to dog day care

Careers *page 37 (CD 1 TRACK 17)*

❈ Dictation 1

1. computer engineer **$47,000 to $65,500**

2. librarian **$43,850**

3. public school teacher **$44,051**

4. accountant **$43,930**

5. lawyer **$90,000 to $150,000**

6. web designer **$47,000 to $65,500**

7. preschool teacher **$15,700 to $23,300**

8. university professor **$51,700 to $82,500**

9. doctor **$100,420 to $260,000**

10. manager and senior executive **$55,890 to $800,000**

and here are some exceptional ones:

11. Vice-President of the U.S. **$171,500**

12. 30-year-old female singer **$30,000,000** (*like Madonna*)

13. professional athlete **$6,750,000** (*football quarterback*)

14. 43-year-old male comedian **$43,000,000** (*like Seinfeld*)

❈ Dictation 2

The father **waved** his hand **scornfully**. He **seemed** to want to tell his son, "You must exercise a little patience and not leap to a decision on something you know nothing about." Then he **remarked**, "It's just as I said. For that reason **it rarely** attracts students from good families. And there's the teaching profession. Do you know anything about teaching or is your information limited to the Teacher's College? It's a miserable profession, **which wins respect from no one**. I'm well **informed** about what's said of such matters, but you're young and inexperienced. **You know nothing of the ways of the world**. It's an occupation uniting people who have modern educations with the products of traditional religious education. It's one utterly devoid of grandeur and esteem. I'm **acquainted with** men of distinction and civil servants who have **flatly refused** to allow their daughters to marry a teacher, **no matter how high his rank**."

The son was sorry but could only repeat with all the politeness and delicacy he could muster, a phrase he had **picked up** in his reading, "**Learning's superior to prestige and wealth**."

The father, Al-Said Ahmad, **looked back and forth** between Kamal and the wardrobe, as though appealing to an invisible person for confirmation of the absurdity of the idea **he had just heard**. Then he said indignantly, "Really? **Have I lived long enough** to hear drivel like this? You imply there's a difference **between prestige and learning**. There's no true knowledge **without prestige and wealth**."

Taxes! Taxes! Taxes! *page 39 (CD 1 TRACK 18)*

❀ Dictation

Americans say that there are only two guarantees in life: **death** and taxes. Of all the rituals of American life, none is more certain than **filling out** yearly tax forms. Compare the **weekly incomes** of these two single women.

(The figures below do not include deductions for insurance or retirement plans.)

	Maria Collins	Suzanne Davis
Income/weekly	$400.00	$1,500.00
Federal Income Tax	**39.00**	**311.00**
State Income Tax	**16.00**	**77.00**
Social Security Tax	**31.00**	**115.00**
Take-home pay	**314.00**	**997.00**

State and Local Taxes

Every state acquires the necessary **revenue** to maintain its government through tax collection, fees, and licenses. The Federal Government also **grants** money to the 50 states. With the revenue that the states receive from the Federal Government, taxes, licenses, and fees, they provide **public services** to their citizens. Examples of these services are public schools, police **protection**, health and **welfare** benefits, and the operation of the state government.

Among the **common types of taxes** that many states impose are personal **income** tax, corporate income tax, **sales tax,** and real **property** tax.

Personal Income Tax

Most states **require** their residents to pay a personal income tax. These states generally use one or two **methods to determine** income tax. These two methods are the **graduated** income tax and the **flat rate** income tax, and both methods require the taxpayer to figure his or her **taxable income**. Massachusetts residents, for example, pay a flat rate of **6%** for the state income tax, but all Americans pay a graduated **federal** income tax. Pity the "**poor**" New Yorker who lives and works in New York City. This person has to pay **three** income taxes: federal, state, and **city taxes**!

State Sales Taxes

A sales tax is **levied** on the sale of goods and services. Very often you pay sales tax when you buy something. The consumer tax system taxes the **retail sale**. The **vendor** at a store collects the tax from the buyer and then sends the **tax money** to the state. The percent of the sales taxes **varies** from state to state. For example, in Massachusetts, it's **5%** and in Hawaii, it's **4%.** So if you bought a car in Massachusetts for $20,000, you'd pay **a total of $21,000**.

What states decide to tax **differs** as well. In some states there is a tax on food, clothing, **medicine**, newspapers, and utilities. In addition, certain groups are often **exempt** from paying sales tax. Religious, educational, and charitable groups are **often excused** from paying sales tax under certain circumstances. A large **portion** of a state's sales tax revenue goes toward **education**, public welfare, and the running of state government. **Because of** this, many states consider the sales tax to be the most important tax **they impose**.

There are a few states that have no sales tax. One such state is **New Hampshire**. But **property taxes** (on houses, factories, and boats) there are **extremely high**.

The Trials of Tipping *page 42 (CD 1 TRACK 19)*

❈ **Dictation**

Tipping says, "<u>**Thank you**</u>," for good service, explains Judy Bowman, president of Protocol Consultants International, who <u>**specializes in**</u> training businesses and corporations in business and <u>**dining etiquette**</u>. According to Bowman, the <u>**standard going rate**</u> for tipping has gone up in the last year, from <u>**15**</u> percent to <u>**20**</u> percent. "If you leave a 10 or 15% tip, you're going to get <u>**raised eyebrows**</u>."

The most important thing to remember about tipping is that you tip members of the <u>**service industry**</u> – people who rely on tips to make a living, <u>**not the management**</u>. Think about your waiter as the guy who sits next to you in economics class and your <u>**tipping outlook**</u> may change. Major tipping situations that people <u>**run into**</u> on a regular basis include trips to the <u>**hair salon**</u>, restaurants, taxis, <u>**bars**</u>, and food delivery services. For each service, a basic tip is required, but it's <u>**up to you**</u> to decide how much to give. For someone who goes <u>**above**</u> and <u>**beyond**</u> the call of duty, you would give a tip closer to the 20% range. For example, when ordering pizza, use the time as a <u>**gauge for tipping**</u>. If you're told the pizza will arrive in 20 minutes, but it comes in 15, you <u>**should tip higher**</u>. On the other hand, if the pizza is late or you've had a <u>**tough time**</u> dealing with the people in the <u>**home**</u> office, you are <u>**completely entitled**</u> to tip <u>**lower**</u> or not at all. If you are not going to tip, <u>**explain why**</u>. This way the delivery guy will know what he's done wrong. The same <u>**rule of thumb**</u> should follow with taxi drivers, hairstylists, and waiters. But if you often go to the same hairstylist or restaurant and the service is good, tip well. The <u>**staff will remember you**</u>!

Hold the Pickles, Hold the Lettuce

page 44 (CD 1 TRACK 20)

❧ Dictation

What is perhaps **most** astonishing about America's fast **food** business is just how successful it **has** become: what began in the 1940s as a handful of hot dog and hamburger stands in Southern California **has** spread like kudzu across the land to become a $110 billion industry. **According to** Eric Schlosser, the author of *Fast Food Nation*, **Americans** now spend more on **fast food than** they spend on higher **education**, personal computers, **computer** software, or new cars, or on movies, books, videos, and recorded music combined. Mr. Schlosser writes that on any given day in the **United States** about one quarter of the adult population visits a fast food **restaurant**, and that the typical **American** now consumes approximately three hamburgers and four orders of French **fries** every week.

"An estimated one of **every** eight workers in the United States has at some time been employed **by** McDonald's," he adds, and the company hires more **people** than any other American organization, public or **private**.

As fast **food** franchises from McDonald's to Pizza **Hut** to Kentucky Fried **Chicken** go global, this dynamic has assumed international flavor. In Brazil, Mr. Schlosser reports, McDonald's **has become** the nation's largest private employer. **Classes** at McDonald's Hamburger University in Oak Park, Illinois, are now taught in 20 different **languages**, and a Chinese anthropologist notes that all the **children** in a primary school in Beijing recognized an image of Ronald McDonald. For the **Chinese**, the anthropologist noted, McDonald's represents "Americana and the promise of modernization."

The People's Court *page 47 (CD 1 TRACK 21)*

❦ Dictation

Case One. Two women gave their **landlord** an $800 **security deposit** before moving into their apartment. When they moved out three years later, the landlord **refused** to return the $800. He said that the women had left **holes** in the walls from **hanging** pictures and **stains** on the carpet. The women claimed the slight damage was from normal **wear** and **tear** of apartment living. In court the landlord produced **bills** totaling $1500 for painting and cleaning he had done.

Case Two. Your local **dry cleaners** lost your winter coat, **valued** at $500, but refused to pay the full **amount** because they say it's only **worth** $200.

Case Three. The auto shop repaired something you didn't **request, charged** you for it, and refused to **release** the car until you paid for it with a **certified** check or cash. You **protested,** but needed your car, so you paid. You demand the **$525** back.

Case Four. The 12-year-old kid next door hit a baseball **through** your window. His parents say it's his responsibility to pay for it. But his weekly **allowance** is $4.00, and it would take three years to **collect** the **full amount**.

Retirement *page 48 (CD 1 TRACK 22)*

❦ Dictation

Jane: And now to our roving reporter, Roger, **who will** bring you a second report on retirement issues.

Roger: Thank you, Jane. In the **first** report on Tuesday night I mentioned that **there were** 2.6 million people **over the age** of 65 working full-**time** and 2.9 working **part**-time. I am here at Adams' Supermarket, one of a six-state chain of supermarkets in the Northeast, and with me is Bob, an employee who has agreed **to be** interviewed. Hello, Bob.

Bob: **Hello, Roger.**

Roger: Can I ask you **how old you are**?

Bob: I'm 73, and I've been working here in the produce department for six **years**. You can see me here 30 **hours a week**.

Roger: Is this what you've **always** done?

Bob: No, I drove a **truck** for the Tropical Banana Company for 32 years, and now I'm stocking **bananas** at Adams' Supermarket. I can't get away from **bananas**.

Roger: So what made you do this?

Bob: I'll tell you, Roger. I **retired** at 65 and for two years I did **nothing**. My wife said I was driving her **crazy**. One **day** I came in here to buy some milk, and I saw someone who looked much **older** than me bagging groceries. I applied for a job and I've been here ever **since**.

Roger: So when do you think you'll give it up?

Bob: Probably when I'm **90** or if I die — whichever comes first. I like feeling that I can still do things and do them well, and now my wife is happy to see me when I come **home**.

Roger: Thank you **very much**, Bob, for speaking with us. The manager of the store **has** told **me** that the Adams' stores have 276 **employees** over 70, 29 **over** 80, and two over **90**, so Bob might get his wish. The manager also said that he wished he had many more older **employees**. He appreciates their life experience and their sense of **responsibility**. I'll be back next Tuesday to talk **about** those workers over 65 for whom retirement is just a dream **because** their nest eggs are falling short.

Childhood *page 51 (CD 1 TRACK 23)*

✤ Dictation 1

<u>**Thirteen-year-old**</u> Tracy has a <u>**stereo, TV**</u>, and <u>**VCR**</u> in her room. Her parents buy her the latest CDs, and they give her a <u>**daily allowance of $10**</u>.

"If I want something, or I need something, I just say '<u>**Can you take me shopping**</u>?'" says the South Boston eighth-grader. "<u>**If I go to the mall with my friends**</u>, my parents give me money. They don't tell me no, really."

Tracy, <u>**however**</u>, says <u>**she's not spoiled**</u>. She does not have a cell phone, <u>**for instance**</u>, unlike many of her friends.

She is the new face <u>**of American teen spending**</u>, a member of a generation that has <u>**grown up**</u> during an era of almost <u>**uninterrupted prosperity**</u>. Nearly a <u>**third of American teenagers carry cell phones**</u>. They eat out <u>**with their friends**</u> at least <u>**once a week**</u>.

The average American teen spent more than <u>**$104**</u> a week in <u>**2001, according to**</u> the marketing research firm Teenage Research Unlimited – <u>**up from $78**</u> just four years earlier. About <u>**two-thirds**</u> of that is money they can spend <u>**however they wish**</u>; the rest is for specific items such as groceries.

That makes teenagers a marketer's dream. But analysts say their spending <u>**habits**</u> — developed during <u>**the late '90s economic boom**</u> — will probably make them <u>**lifetime spendthrifts**</u>. Some worry that the intense adolescent focus on consuming will <u>**bring about**</u> a future in which an even greater number of Americans are living <u>**beyond their means**</u>.

❀ Dictation 2

In contrast, there are many children in the world who are engaged in extreme and hazardous forms of work, and who are being robbed of their fundamental right to a childhood.

It is estimated that about **120** million children between the ages of **5 and 14** work at least full-time. If children for whom work is a **secondary activity** are **included**, the figure reaches **250 million**. Sixty-one percent of these were in **Asia,** **32%** in Africa, and **7%** in Latin America. Most working children in **rural areas** were found in **agriculture; urban** children worked in **trade** and services, with fewer in **manufacturing, construction**, and **domestic service**.

Conditions of child labor range from that of four-year-olds **tied** to rug looms to keep them from running away, to seventeen-year-olds **helping out** on the family farm. In some cases, a child's work can be **helpful** to him or her and to the family; **working and earning** can be a positive experience in a child's **growing up**. This depends largely on the age of the child, the conditions in which the child works, and whether work **prevents the child from going to school**. In addition, more than **300,000** children, some **as young as 10**, are child soldiers and are **waging war** in **40** different **conflicts** around the world.

Chinese New Year *page 54 (CD 1 TRACK 24)*

❀ Dictation

In feudal times, the Chinese believed that the eve of the New Year marked the Kitchen God's departure to heaven **in order to report on the household**. To welcome the Kitchen God **back to the home** in the New Year, each family feasted and performed a "spring-cleaning." The spring festival symbolized **a fresh start** and the earth's seasonal return to life.

"We serve **special dishes** that are auspicious for the New Year," Danny Woo, the manager at the Jumbo Seafood Restaurant in **Chinatown**, says. He is planning an **eight-course special dinner**, because eight in Chinese **is a lucky number**, since it sounds like the word "**prosper**."

Chicken and fish are made only in their whole form to represent a year **that starts without missing pieces**.

One traditional Chinese **recipe** for the New Year is Clams in Black Bean **Sauce**, because their **shells** resemble Chinese coins, which **symbolize prosperity**. Another **traditional** recipe is Good Luck Dumplings.

❀ Pair Dictation

Good Luck Dumplings

Ingredients

    1 lb. (pound) pork, beef, or tofu, drained of excess liquid
    1/4 teaspoon salt
    1 clove minced garlic
    1 teaspoon minced fresh ginger root
    1/4 teaspoon pepper
    2 tablespoons sesame oil
    1 cup chopped green onions
    1-2 packages of wonton wrappers
    Vegetables of your choice

Love Votes *page 57 (CD 1 TRACK 25)*

❈ Dictation

1. You've **accepted a date** when someone you REALLY like calls you **up** and **asks** you **out** for the same night. You try to **get out of** the first date.

2. You **find out** that your spouse is infertile. You really want children of your own and cannot **accept adoption**. You leave your spouse.

3. Your favorite sister is **engaged to** marry a man who, in your opinion, is **bad news**. She is in love. You try to talk her **out of it**.

4. You have a serious long-distance romance in your country. To relieve **loneliness**, you start a romantic **friendship** locally. You **bring up** your commitment to the local person.

5. Your teenage daughter is dating a man of another **race**. You try to **break** them **up**.

6. In order to **marry** someone you love, you must **give up** your **religion** and change to theirs. You do it.

7. You give your mate a gift **worth** $200, then you **break up** a month **later**. You ask **for it back**.

8. You've been **going out with** a person who loves you much more than you love them. You've been **up front** about your feelings but your mate doesn't care. You end the **relationship** now in order to **spare** them a greater **hurt** later.

Independence Day *page 58 (CD 1 TRACK 26)*

❈ Dictation 1

1. France	a. July 4. 1776
2. United States of America	b. **September 7, 1822**
3. Brazil	c. **July 1, 1867**
4. Australia	d. **July 14, 1789**
5. Canada	e. **January 26, 1901**

Answers: France, d.
U.S.A., a.
Brazil, b
Australia, e
Canada, c

❀ Dictation 2

<u>**July 4,**</u> the anniversary of the day the Declaration of Independence was signed, is a day in the United States **that everyone looks forward to**. About a week before the celebration, you will see small and large flags flying, and stores beginning to display **red**, **white**, and **blue decorations**.

In almost every little town across the country, there is a parade. People line the route **cheering and waving little flags.** The parade often begins with a line of **antique cars** dating from the nineteen twenties and thirties, followed by **old soldiers** marching and playing patriotic songs like "Yankee Doodle Dandy." Even **in the age of** dazzling technology, Americans like to **maintain the tradition** of an old-fashioned parade.

In the afternoon, friends and family will gather for a **picnic or** barbecue. At one time, fresh salmon and fresh peas were part of a **traditional menu**, but the **barbecue** lends itself to chicken, steaks, and hot dogs, **all-time American favorites**.

Everyone waits for dark, **when the fireworks begin**. Most large cities have extravagant concerts and firework displays. In Boston, on the Esplanade by the Charles River, **350,000 plus people** will gather to watch and hear the Boston Pops. Some of the crowd **will have gotten up** at 6:00 A.M. to get good seats for this great show. The crowd will **sing along** to the well-known songs, and a popular star will read the Declaration of Independence while **the orchestra plays** in the background. The last piece, Tchaikovsky's 1812 Overture, will include real cannons firing. This is the traditional ending, and the crowd cheers as the orchestra plays **its last notes**. Finally the moment arrives, and you can hear the crowd's oohs and aahs as the sensational half-hour of fireworks **begins to light up the sky** with red, white, and blue shells that burst **and then float gently down to earth**.

Do You Believe in Ghosts? *page 60 (CD 2 TRACK 1)*

❀ Dictation 1

If you'd like to visit some places in the United States that have a reputation **for being haunted**, you can buy the book, *The **National Directory** of Haunted Places*, by Dennis Hauck, a well-known **authority** on paranormal phenomena. The book contains several thousand **carefully researched** places in countries around the world and mentions many **spooky houses** in the United States.

The most **famous ghost** in the White House in Washington, D.C., one that **has been seen** by presidents and their families on many occasions, is **Abraham Lincoln**, the 16th president, who **was assassinated** in 1865. Lincoln had many tragedies **in his personal life,** one of which was the death of his son, Willie, at age 11. Lincoln believed **in the afterlife** and tried several times to **contact** his son through seances in the White House. Lincoln also had **premonitions** of his own death and once told his secretary that **he knew he** was going to die in office and that he could **envision** his casket in the Rotunda Room of the White House. *Note to teachers:* After this unit you may want to play the song or video "Ghostbusters."

❀ Dictation 2: Judge for Yourself

Madame Zelda was a **psychic** who **claimed** she was able to read people's auras and predict the future. However, after she **underwent** some tests at the hospital and **was given** a CAT scan, she **insisted** that it **affected** her abilities. She **asserted** that she was no longer able to read auras, **foresee coming events,** or even help the police find missing persons as she **had** in the past. Every time she **used** her psychic powers, she just **got headaches**. She **sued** the hospital.

❀ The Verdict

The jury **ruled FOR** Madame Zelda and **awarded** her **$1 million**. However, the judge, who **had** the final word, **overturned** the decision and **threw out** the verdict.

Election Day in the U.S.A. *page 62 (CD 2 TRACK 2)*

Answers for questions in the introduction

1. November   2. Every 4 years   3. 8 years

❈ Dictation

In the United States, presidential **elections** are held every four years. They are always **held** on the first Tuesday after the first Monday in the month of **November**. In most states, Election Day is not a holiday from **work** or school. The President and the Vice-President are **elected** for four years. Only natural born **citizens** of the United States are **allowed** to be President. Presidents are **required** to be at least thirty-five years old.

There are two major political **parties**, the Democratic Party **and** the Republican Party. The vice-presidential **candidates** are selected by the presidential candidates. Both people are nominated by their **political** parties at a national convention several months **before** Election Day.

On Election Day, **millions** of Americans go to the polls to **vote**. Polls are **located** in schools, churches, and public buildings. Polls are **open** from early in the morning until 7:00 or 8:00 in the **evening**. Most polls use a **voting** machine. People always **vote** by secret ballot.

Today, all United States **citizens** 18 and **older** can vote if they want to. In presidential elections, **about** 75% of Americans vote. On election night the votes are tabulated by **computer**, and the winner is usually **announced** by midnight.

❈ Discussion

To the teacher:

1. Column A. There are no correct answers here. Accept different opinions. Just get them to explain why they decided on each one. The purpose is to get them to talk.

2. Column B. Answers will vary according to who is in office. Explain to students that Democrats and Republicans may both want to improve education but have different ideas on how that is done.

The Olympic Games *page 65 (CD 2 TRACK 3)*

Note to teachers: In the prediction section, accept any words that are logical and grammatical.

❀ The Ancient Games

Ancient Greece gave birth to the Olympics more than 2000 years **ago** in 776 B.C. The Games ended in 394 A.D. During those 1000 years, the Ancient Games **were** festivals to honor the many gods that Greeks **worshiped**. Olympia, the town where the most powerful god, Zeus, was worshiped, **held** the first Olympics. The first Olympic Games consisted of no more than **one** foot race, but as the Games **became** more popular, other events were **added**, such as horse racing, boxing, chariot racing, and wrestling.

Young men of wealth dominated the early Games, but later, as other sports festivals became more and more popular and offered big cash **prizes** to winners, men of all **classes** of society could make sports a **full-time** career. The Olympic Games never offered cash prizes; it was the **glory** of winning that meant everything to young men ages 12-17.

❀ The Modern Games

The Olympics were **revived** in 1896 and were held every four years. The Modern Games were later **divided** into the Winter and **Summer** Games. Now the Winter and Summer Games alternate every two **years**. Fewer countries and sports are represented at the Winter Games because fewer **athletes** come from countries with high mountains and snow fields. The Summer Games **attract** thousands of athletes from over 200 countries and include many more types of sports, **such as** swimming and running. Many Olympic athletes today think of the Olympics as more than just **winning** the gold, silver, or bronze **medal**. They **believe** that doing your personal best brings respect and understanding for **all** athletes playing the same game for peace **and** humanity.

Teacher's Note: John Lennon's "Imagine" is a good song to play for this unit.

Birthdays around the World *page 68 (CD 2 TRACK 4)*

❈ Dictation

Germany. Germans take birthdays **seriously**, sometimes receiving a **half-day** vacation from work. Flowers and wine are **common gifts**.

Japan. The birthday child wears **entirely** new clothes to **mark** the occasion. Certain birthdays are more important than others. For example, usually only the birthdays of **60, 70, 79, 88,** and **99** rate gifts.

United States. A cake is made, and **candles** are **put on top**, based on how old the person is. After everyone sings the "happy birthday" song, the person makes a wish and **blows out** the candles. If they blow them all out with one blow, their birthday **wish will come true**.

Denmark. A **flag** is **flown** outside a window to **designate** that someone who lives in that house **is having** a birthday. **Presents** are placed around the **child's bed** while they are sleeping so they will see them **immediately upon awakening**.

England. When you reach **80,** 90, or **100** years of age, you receive a **telegram** from the Queen. (In the U.S., when you **reach 100**, you receive a letter from the **President**.)

China. Age **30** is considered **becoming** an **adult**, and there is usually **quite a celebration**. Birthdays are traditionally celebrated for adults who **have reached** at least 60 years of **age**. Lo mein noodles are often **served**.

Mexico. The piñata, usually made out of paper maché and in the **form** of an animal, is filled with **goodies** and hung from the **ceiling**. Children **take turns** hitting the piñata so candy and small toys **spill out** for everyone to share. Also, when a daughter is **15**, the birthday is celebrated with a special **mass in her honor**. A party is then given to **introduce** her to everyone as a young woman. The father dances a **waltz with her**.

Ireland. The birthday child is **lifted** upside down and "**bumped**" on the floor for good luck. The number of bumps **given** is the age of the child plus one for **extra good luck**.

Note: Check out this site: http://www.kidsparties.com/traditions.htm

Golden Wedding Anniversary *page 70 (CD 2 TRACK 5)*

❀ Dictation

The Clarks were **looking forward to** June 20th, when their **six** sons, and their sons' wives and children, were coming to their Utah home for an **anniversary celebration** organized by their son **Ron.** Everyone was **due** to arrive by **June 19**. Each couple had **one**, **two**, or **three** children. From the following clues, can you match the sons with their wives, determine how many children each couple had, **deduce** their time of **arrival**, and **figure out** where each family lived?

1. One couple **crossed** no state or national borders in **getting to** the homecoming.
2. The couples **arrived June 19** at **8 A.M., 10 A.M., noon, 2 P.M., 3 P.M.**, and **5 P.M.**
3. The couples from **Germany** and **Japan have** the same number of children.
4. George **has** only one child, a boy. Eileen has only two girls, and Carol **has** only one girl.
5. The son from **Texas arrived** at **10 A. M.**
6. Pat, who hails from Wyoming, **has** three children and did not arrive either first or last.
7. Frank **flew in** from **Germany** and **arrived** after **noon**, two hours after his brother from Japan.
8. Bert and Bob don't **have** the same number of children. The son from Texas **has** one **less** child than the son from Wyoming. The son from Arizona **has** one more child than Frank.
9. Wendy **arrived** after Jill, who **arrived** after Linda. But Linda **arrived** before Eileen, who **arrived** before **noon**.
10. Keith **drove** all night and **arrived** before **10 A.M.** with his three hungry children.
11. Bert **packed** his wife and two children into the car that morning and **arrived** three hours after Frank.

❀ Solution

Keith and Linda from Utah arrived at 8 A.M. with three children.
Ron and Eileen arrived from Texas at 10 A.M. with two children.
George and Jill arrived from Japan at 12 noon with one child.
Frank and Carol arrived from Germany at 2 P.M. with one child.
Bob and Pat arrived from Wyoming at 3 P.M. with three children.
Bert and Wendy arrived from Arizona at 5 P.M. with two children.

You Be the Judge *page 72 (CD 2 TRACK 6)*

❁ Dictation

Case 1. New York

A driver who was **racing** down the street at **100 miles per hour** crashed into a limousine **carrying** a wedding party. **Instantly** killed were the groom, age 27, and his brother, age 29, who was the **best man.** The bride, age 24, died 18 days later **without knowing** of her husband's death. The driver of the car that killed them was **sentenced** to **three** years in prison.

Case 2. Texas

A man got into an argument with a police officer and **bit off** part of the officer's ear. The man was sentenced to **10** years in prison.

Case 3. Massachusetts

A 14-year old girl was **raped** by a 38-year-old man. She said that her life would never be the same again. The judge told her to "**get over it**" and sentenced the man to **6** months in prison.

Email Spam *page 73 (CD 2 TRACK 7)*

❦ Dictation

Note: The email addresses and telephone numbers are not real.

1. Subject: A Guaranteed University **Diploma**!
   From: Educate@COLLdip.741.pm

   Do you want to earn the **respect** in your **community** that you've always wanted? You can receive a **bachelor's**, master's, or doctorate diploma from us and hang it on your office wall! Our president will **automatically** accept you through our **open admissions** policy! There are no exams to take, classes to **attend**, or textbooks to buy. We award all levels of diplomas from well-known, **non-accredited** universities in any field of study you wish, including engineering, teaching, computers, **business**, or any other **discipline**. Just call 1-814-453-2312 any time.

2. Subject: **Lose It Fast**!
   From: Weightloss@diet.761.vn

   You can lose one pound a **week** on Dr. Mayer's simple and quick **no-pill** diet. You can go from **size 16 to 14** in one week! After the second week on this diet your clothes will be **falling off**, and you'll have to go out and buy a new **wardrobe**! Call today: 1-309-987-8876. Only $**49.99**!

Be sure that these warnings come up during the discussion of question #4.

1. Never disclose sensitive information such as Soc. Sec. numbers, bank names, PIN codes, credit card numbers, or account numbers of any kind over e-mail.

2. Never accept offers from, or send money to, any individual or organization not known to you.

3. Read all email carefully. If an offer sounds too good to be true, it probably is.

Questions about Appearance *page 74 (CD 2 TRACK 8)*

❀ Dictation 1

School administrators are girding **for a fashion showdown in school corridors** as racy and revealing back-to school fashions inspired by navel-baring pop stars like Christina Aguilera and Britney Spears **flood clothing retailers**.

While teen fashion tastes have long clashed with adult preferences, principals say the abundance of skin-revealing styles for girls this year threatens to have **students arriving dressed for rock concerts, not for the classroom**.

Last year the F.A. Day Middle School in Newton clarified the school's dress code, **adding specifics about covering the stomach** and **hips**. But the code is only a "recommendation" because the school is unclear about **the legality of regulating dress at all**, said the principal, Paul Stein. The matter, school officials say, is complicated **by questions of personal taste**, First Amendment rights, **sensitive issues of female body image**, and the tricky reality that the same outfit may look plain on one girl **and provocative on another**.

❀ Dictation 2: Judge for Yourself

In Alaska, a lawyer, **while pleading a case,** was asked by the judge **to wear a suit and tie** rather than the more casual attire of a **flannel shirt and jeans** he was wearing. **When the lawyer refused to alter** his mode of dress, he was held in contempt of court. The lawyer challenged the contempt citation, arguing that it violated his constitutional right of privacy and liberty **to choose his own style of dress**. Also, **it discriminated against men**.

❀ The Verdict

The court ruled **against** the lawyer, stating that the court **had the right to establish a minimum code** and that a **coat and tie** fell within a **reasonable standard of dress**. **As to the question of discrimination**, the court required women **to wear conservative business clothing,** which made **the standard the same**.

❀ Dictation 3: Judge for Yourself

Albert had grown his hair to 10 inches **in preparation for his special hairstyle**. He went to the hair salon bearing a photograph of the style he wanted. **After the haircut, he was furious** because the stylist had cut the hair on top of his head **far too short**. He was ridiculed by his friends and had to resort to **wearing a baseball cap all the time**. He went to a psychiatrist for help. He sued the salon **for $10,000** in damages.

❀ The Verdict

The court **ruled against** Albert and **dismissed** the case because the court **held** that the hair **can easily be grown back**.

Cheating in College *page 77 (CD 2 TRACK 9)*

❀ Dictation

1. Cheating in the classroom isn't just about **copying** someone's paper or writing answers on a **crib sheet**. With the **internet**, cheating has gone **high tech**.

2. **Hundreds** of web sites offer **term** papers, class notes, and exams. Students may pay **up to $350** for a research paper bought through the internet.

3. **Plagiarism** is the most common form of cheating, and university professors admit that it is **hard to catch**. It depends **on the vigilance** of faculty members and a certain **degree of luck**.

4. More than **75%** of 2000 students from **21** colleges nationwide **admitted to cheating** last year.

5. Experts say that most students cheat because of **grade pressure**.

6. **Research** on college cheating shows that men and women **equally** admitted to **academic** dishonesty; business and **engineering** majors were most likely to cheat, **compared with** other majors.

7. Colleges are doing more **to prevent** cheating, and universities work with international students who come from **cultures** that allow **citing** another person's work **without quotation** marks or footnotes.

8. At some schools, possible **punishment for cheating** includes **expulsion**, but most professors simply give the student an **F in the course**.

What Would You Do If . . .? *page 79 (CD 2 TRACK 10)*

❀ Dictation

1. One hot summer afternoon, while **walking through** a parking lot at a mall, you notice a dog **suffering** badly from the heat inside a **locked car**. What would you do? Anything?

2. If you went to a dinner party at your **boss's** house and were **offered** some food you had never tried (which looked awful) would you try it **even if** it looked **strange** or **smelled weird**?

3. Which sex has **an easier life** in your culture, male or female? Have you ever **wished** that you were of the **opposite sex**?

4. You are driving late at night in a safe but **deserted** neighborhood when a cat suddenly **darts** in front of your car. You **slam on** the brakes, but you hit the cat. Would you stop to see how **injured** the cat was? If you did and **found** that the cat was **dead** but had a **name tag**, would you **contact the owner**?

5. Would you ever **consider taking** a week-long vacation **alone**? If yes, where would you go and what would you do?

6. Would you **rather** play a game with someone **more or less talented** than you? Why or why not?

7. Would you like **to be famous** some day? Why or why not?

8. If someone **offered** you a **pill** that made you immortal, would you take it? (The pill is free, has no **side effects**, and could also be given to any **number of** people of your **choosing**.)

Short Business Decisions *page 81 (CD 2 TRACK 11)*

❅ **Dictation**

1. A valuable breakthrough <u>**has been recently made by**</u> one of your competitors. It is going to improve <u>**the quality of his product**</u> and reduce <u>**the cost of production**</u>. Your product will become uncompetitive. Someone comes to you and offers <u>**to sell you**</u> <u>**details**</u> of your competitor's research, which led to his technical breakthrough. <u>**What do**</u> <u>**you do**</u>?

2. Your company has recently acquired <u>**a villa in Spain**</u> as part of the assets of a merger. You are hoping to sign <u>**an important contract**</u> with the local government. You <u>**hear that**</u> <u>**the wife**</u> of their chief negotiator <u>**is ill**</u> and needs to spend the winter in a <u>**warm, dry**</u> <u>**climate.**</u> Do you offer him the use <u>**of your empty villa in Spain**</u>?

3. Your company needs <u>**to hire a senior executive**</u> for an overseas subsidiary. After interviewing the candidates <u>**the best candidate, by far,**</u> is a <u>**35-year-old woman**</u>. Her husband is a <u>**writer**</u> and they have <u>**two children**</u>. She is a very valuable member of your staff, and she <u>**has made it known**</u> that she may leave the company if <u>**she is not given**</u> <u>**this position**</u>. <u>**On the other hand,**</u> as a woman, she <u>**might not be**</u> well received by the company that she would be working for. This might affect <u>**the volume of business**</u> done by your company. <u>**What do you do**</u>?

4. The peak sales time <u>**for your company's product**</u> is always in the <u>**three months before**</u> <u>**Christmas**</u>. In October you find a <u>**minor fault**</u> in the product. It is not <u>**dangerous**</u> but <u>**will shorten**</u> the normal life of the product. Withdrawing it <u>**at this time**</u> would mean losing your sales. Would you recommend withdrawing it right now?

Workplace Ethics *page 83 (CD 2 TRACK 12)*

❀ Dictogloss

1. Your business venture fails and you owe your creditors $15,000. You can avoid payment by declaring bankruptcy. Do you?

2. An official of a large company demands a payment in return for giving you a lucrative contract. Do you pay?

3. You make long distance calls as part of your work for a middle-sized firm. Do you make private calls if you know they cannot be traced?

4. You are planning to quit in five months when your boss suddenly gives you a high-paying management job. You still intend to quit. Do you tell your boss now?

5. A friend who needs a job applies at your business. Someone who is better qualified also applies. Do you hire your friend?

❀ Dictation: Judge for Yourself

Todd was the executor **of his underage niece's estate** because **she had been left in his care** after his sister and her husband were killed. **Todd was a gambler** and learned of "a sure thing" in a horserace. He borrowed **$5000 from his niece's account** to place the bet. Todd won **and doubled his money**. He returned the **$5000** to the account and kept the rest. **When** what he had done **was discovered**, a friend of his niece helped her sue for the winnings.

❀ The Verdict

The court **ruled against** Todd. **Not only** did he have **to return** the winnings, **but** the court **also relieved** him of his **duties** as an executor for his niece.

What's So Funny? *page 85 (CD 2 TRACK 13)*

❧ Dictation

Note to teachers: If there is any vocabulary you think the students don't know, review it ahead of time. Some may not know what "puppy" means.

1. A woman got on a bus **holding a baby**. The bus driver said, "That's **the ugliest baby** I've ever seen. In a huff, the woman **slammed** her fare into the fare box and took an **aisle** seat in the **rear** of the bus. The man **seated** next to her sensed that she was **agitated** and asked her what **was wrong**. "The bus driver **insulted me**." The man **sympathized** and said: "Why, he's a **public servant** and shouldn't say things to insult **passengers**." "You're right," she said. "I think I'll go back up there and give him a **piece** of **my mind**." "That's a good idea," the man said. "Here, let me hold **your monkey**."

2. A guy goes to a psychiatrist because he hasn't been feeling **mentally well**. When the psychiatrist asks him to **describe** what is wrong, the guy tells him that he has been feeling "**like a dog**" lately. The psychiatrist then asks his **patient**, "How long have you been feeling this way?" The guy **replies**, "Ever since I **was a puppy**."

3. A person who speaks two languages is **bilingual**.
   A person who speaks three languages is **trilingual**.
   A person who speaks four languages is **multilingual**.
   What is a person who speaks one language? "**An American**."

Riddles

   1. C   2. A   3. E   4. F   5. B   6. D

More Riddles

   1. C   2. E   3. D   4. B   5. A

Note: A resource is the TESL Journal web site — http:/iteslj.org/c/jokes-long.html

Limericks and Tongue Twisters *page 87 (CD 2 TRACK 14)*

✽ Dictation

Note to teachers:

> For best results, be sure students know the meaning of words like "squid," "defiant," etc.

1. There once was an old man from Nesser

   Whose knowledge grew lesser and lesser.

   It at last grew so small,

   He knew nothing at all,

   And now he's a college professor!

2. There was a young fellow named Sid

   Who loved to go fishing for squid.

   But he caught quite a giant

   Who was very defiant,

   And ate Sid all up, yes it did. (Poor kid.)

You can also use limericks as strip stories by cutting up each line and have students work in pairs to figure out the poem. The internet has dozens of limerick web sites.

The New World Language *page 89 (CD 2 TRACK 15)*

❀ Dictation 1

It is everywhere. **Some 380 million people speak** it as their first language and perhaps two thirds as many again as their second. **A billion are learning it**. About a third of the world's population are in some sense exposed to it, and by 2050, it is predicted, **half the world will be more or less** proficient in it. It is the language of globalization – of international business, politics, and diplomacy. It is the language of computers and the internet. You'll see it on posters in Cote d'Ivoire, **you'll hear it in pop songs in Tokyo**, and you'll read it in official documents in Phnom Penh. Deutsche Welle broadcasts in it. Bjork, an Icelander, **sings in it**. French business schools teach in it. It is the medium of expression in cabinet meetings in Bolivia. Truly, the tongue spoken back in the **1300s** only by the "low people" of England **has come a long way**. It is now the global language. **How come? Not because English is easy**. True, genders are simple, since English relies on "it" as the pronoun for all inanimate nouns, reserving masculine for *bona fide* males and feminine for females (and countries and ships). **But the verbs tend to be irregular**, the grammar **bizarre**, and the match between **spelling** and **pronunciation** a nightmare. English is now so **widely spoken in so many places** that umpteen versions have evolved, some so peculiar that "native" speakers may have trouble understanding each other.

❀ Dictation 2

1. They are too **close** to the door to **close** it.
2. There was a **row** among the oarsmen about how to **row**.
3. I shed a **tear** about the **tear** in my new shirt.
4. A farm can **produce produce**.
5. The dump was so full, it had to **refuse refuse**.
6. The **present** is a good time to **present** the **present**.
7. The insurance for the **invalid** was **invalid**.
8. The bandage was **wound** around the **wound**.
9. The soldier decided to **desert** in the **desert**.

❀ Dictation 3

An international exchange student **is hanging out with his new group of friends** at a party. He is confident in his ability to hold a conversation with everyone, **even crack a joke or two**. Then someone offers one of his friends a drink. The friend replies, "Um, like, no, I'm like O.K." The student thinks, "That **wasn't in my textbook**."

Slang and filler speech is so ingrained in **our everyday conversation**. The word "like" has infiltrated so many young minds that no sentence is left untouched by these "non-fluencies."

The trend is not new. Since the 70s, California's "valley-girl" talk has plagued America's youth **from coast to coast**.

According to Professor Richard Katula of Northeastern University's communications studies department, these filler words allow teenagers who feel vulnerable expressing their beliefs a "way out."

He translated the use of "like" as "what I just said, I may not mean." These filler words are referred to as negative speech, **or not thinking before speaking**. Those interjected "likes" give unsure youths a moment to soften or manipulate what could have otherwise been a strong, personal, confrontational statement. Often the result is **that the students sound less intelligent**.

Trivia Contest *page 92 (CD 2 TRACK 16)*

Note to teachers.

1. You can change this dictation to accommodate the interests of your class. For example, the first question is: How many people are there in _____ _____? This answer key will give "the world" but you may want to change it to: New York or Los Angeles. It can be a review of noun clause usage.

2. You can make up your own list of trivia questions. Use information you have covered in previous classes or from recent newspaper reports that they might remember.

❈ **Answer key**

1. How many people are there in **the world**? 6 billion

2. Where are most American cars **manufactured** in the United States?   Detroit

3. **How often** are presidential **elections held** in the U.S.? every 4 years

4. Who wrote The ***Adventures*** *of Huckleberry **Finn***? Mark Twain

5. What does **B.L.T.** mean? bacon, lettuce, and tomato sandwich

6. Where can you buy a **whopper junior**?   at Burger King

7. Who is the **richest woman** in the world?   Queen Elizabeth II

8. In what year did Americans **first land** on the moon? 1969

9. What is the **most common** first name in the world? Mohammed

10. What is the **best-selling** ice cream **flavor** in the U.S.? Vanilla

11. How long has your teacher **taught** in this program?

Who Would Say That? *page 93 (CD 2 TRACK 17)*

❦ Dictation

1. It's a 1999 and in perfect **condition**. And it only has **50,000** miles.
   Speaker: Used car salesman or someone trying to sell his car through an ad.

2. Do you have any **spare change**?
   Speaker: Beggar or street person.

3. We expect to be **taking off** in about ten minutes.
   Speaker: Pilot.

4. I think that "Snoopy" should go **on a diet**.
   Speaker: Veterinarian

5. Ugga mugga hubba **hooba** goolak.
   Speaker: Accept any possible answers, e.g. someone who lived 1,000,000 years ago.

6. Would you like to try something different this time? A **perm**? Or a **frost**?
   Speaker: Hair stylist

7. I **predict** that next year you'll meet the perfect man and get **married**.
   Speaker: Fortune teller – or card reader

8. It's a **home run** for Reggie. Now it's **tied** two to two.
   Speaker: Baseball game announcer

9. May I see your driver's license and **registration**, please?
   Speaker: Police officer

10. It's a beautiful **top floor** two-bedroom.
    Speaker: Real estate agent

11. **Open wide**.
    Speaker: Dentist or dental hygienist

12. The **fine** is 10 cents a day for each one that is **overdue**.
    Speaker: Librarian

Don't Be Fooled! *page 94 (CD 2 TRACK 18)*

❀ Dictation

1. Mary Jones was born on December 27th, **yet** her birthday is always **in the summer**. How can this be?

   Answer: She's from a country south of the equator.

2. Frank was walking down Main Street when it started to **rain**. He did not have an umbrella and he wasn't wearing a hat. His clothes **were soaked**, yet not a hair on his head **got wet**. How could this happen?

   Answer: He is bald.

3. There is an **ancient invention** still used in parts of the world today that **allows** people to see through **walls**. What is it?

   Answer: A window.

4. A taxi driver took a group of **passengers** to the train station. The station is **normally** an hour away, but with terrible traffic, it took a full hour and **a half**. On the return trip, the traffic was still as **heavy** and yet it took only **90** minutes. Why?

   Answer: 90 minutes is the same as one and a half hours.

5. Do they have a fourth of July **in England**?

   Answer: Yes, but it's not a holiday.

6. Some months have **30** days; others have 31 days. How many have **28** days?

   Answer: All of them.

7. What five-letter word becomes **shorter** when you add **two letters** to it?

   Answer: Short.

8. A farmer had **fifteen horses**. **All but nine** died. How many did he have left?

   Answer: 9.

9. A woman from New York **married** ten different men from that city, yet she didn't **break any laws.** None of the men **died** and she **never divorced**. How was this possible?

   Answer: The woman was a minister.

10. Which one of the following words **does not belong** with the others and why? Father, Aunt, Sister, **Cousin**, Mother, Uncle

    Answer: Cousin. All the others refer to a specific sex.

Riddles

1. d   2. a   3. b   4. c

Learning Styles *page 95 (CD 2 TRACK 19)*

❊ **Dictation**

Here is a description of one kind of learner, **the logical learner**. These children are very mathematically inclined. **They enjoy problems**, particularly if they are **math related**. They are **similar to** Mr. Spock on "Star Trek," in that they are very logical, straightforward types of learners. They will plague you with questions **on how things work**, how things relate to one another, and **why things are here**. Their **favorite toys** as young children were building blocks and pattern puzzles. **Answer their ongoing questions** with as much patience as you can muster, and one day they may become engineers.

In order to determine what kind of a learner you are, psychologists will give you a learning style inventory test. Here are some examples of the type of question you may be asked. You will be asked to check the statements that are true about you.

_____ I prefer to **fiddle** with things while I listen or talk to people.

_____ I prefer to **read a map** rather than listen to someone giving me directions.

_____ I **gesture** a lot when I explain things.

_____ I enjoy doing more **than one thing at a time**.

_____ I often **nibble** while I study.

_____ When I read, **I often fidget** and try to "feel" the content or even act out parts of what I read.

What Used To Be *page 98 (CD 2 TRACK 20)*

✿ Dictation

Part A

1. Before **electricity**, people used to . . .

2. The country that is now called **Thailand** . . . .

3. Before **word processors**, people used to . . .

4. **Millions** of years ago. . .

5. Before doctors became **licensed, barbers** used to . . .

6. In many **ancient** and not so ancient cultures. . .

7. Before the car was **invented**, people used to . . .

8. The country that **used to be** called Ceylon. . .

9. People used to think that **potatoes** . . .

10. Before **television**, people used to . . .

Part B

Before electricity, people used to read by candlelight.

The country that is now called Thailand used to be called Siam.

Before word processors, people used to use typewriters.

Millions of years ago, dinosaurs used to roam the earth.

Before doctors became licensed, barbers used to perform some operations.

In many ancient and not so ancient cultures, people used to have slaves.

Before the car was invented, people used to travel by horse.

The country that used to be called Ceylon is now called Sri Lanka.

People used to think that potatoes were poisonous.

Before television, people used to read more.

All About Weather *page 99 (CD 2 TRACK 21)*

❀ Dictation 1

Joke One

I had just moved north and was feeling apprehensive about the severity of the winters. My anxious questions about the weather brought this reply from a native. "Ma'am, we have four seasons here: early winter, midwinter, late winter, and next winter."

Joke Two

The Michaels family owned a small farm in Canada just yards away from the North Dakota border. Their land had been the subject of a minor dispute between Canada and the United States for generations. Mrs. Michaels, who had just celebrated her ninetieth birthday, lived on the farm with her son and three grandchildren. One day, her son came into her room holding a letter. "I just got some news, Mom," he said. "The government has come to an agreement with the people in Washington. They've decided that our land is really part of the United States. We have the right to approve or disapprove of the agreement. What do you think?" "What do I think?" his mother said. "Jump at it! Call them right now and tell them we accept. I don't think I could stand another one of those Canadian winters."

❀ Dictation 2

1. It was a **mixed bag** of precipitation.
2. It's raining **cats and dogs**.
3. I'll take **a rain check**.
4. Don't rain **on my parade**.
5. I can **weather** the storm.
6. I'm **under the weather**.
7. It was a real **snow job**.
8. I was **snowed under** with work.
9. The problems **snowballed** by the hour.
10. I was **thunderstruck**.
11. The idea came **out of the blue**.
12. She was **on cloud nine**.
13. Her head was **in the clouds**.

Facts about Drinking *page 102 (CD 2 TRACK 22)*

❦ Dictation

Note to teachers: The legal drinking age is 21 in all states.

1. Some people can drink a lot without **ever getting** drunk. **False.**

   (*Depending on many factors, the reaction to alcohol is somewhat different for most people. However, people who drink large quantities of alcohol without showing much reaction have often built up a tolerance to it. This is known as an addiction. Also, the brain is still affected; reaction times are still erratic, judgment is impaired, e.g. other cars may seem farther away to a driver than they usually are.*)

2. Approximately 40% of **fatal** highway accidents are **alcohol related**. **True.**

3. **Switching drinks** will make you drunker than staying with one kind of alcohol. **False.**

   (*The drinks can make you sick but not drunker. What causes an adverse reaction to alcohol is drinking too much, not the type of alcohol.*)

4. You can **coat the stomach** with milk or food to slow down the rate of intoxication. **True.**

5. The best way to **sober up** is to drink coffee and take a cold shower. **False.**

   (*If you drink coffee, you'll be awake but drunk. If you take a cold shower, you'll be clean but drunk. The best way is to sit and wait because the body metabolizes 1/2 ounce of pure alcohol an hour, and there is no way to speed up this process.*)

6. **Safety** experts say that one out of every two Americans will **be victimized by** a drunk driver. **True.**

7. A person **can overdose** on alcohol. **True.**

   (*There are about 1000 recorded alcohol overdose deaths a year; many are college students.*)

8. It is easy **to spot** an alcoholic. **False.**

   (*Nearly 10% of the population has a drinking problem. Ten million people in the U.S. are dependent on alcohol; many hold responsible jobs and are raising families. 40% are college graduates. At the same time, an alcoholic's life expectancy is shortened by 10-12 years.*)

9. Drinking during pregnancy can affect the **unborn child**. **True.**

10. Most alcoholics are **middle-aged** or older. **False.**

    (*The highest proportion of drinking problems occur with men in their early 20s. Among those age groups surveyed by the National Survey on Drug Abuse [12-17, 18-25, and 26 and over] abuse was more prevalent among those 18-25.*)

11. Children of alcoholics are <u>**more likely**</u> to develop alcoholism. **True.**

(Research indicates that sons have a 1 in 3 chance of developing alcoholism because, like diabetes, it is a genetic disease.)

12. <u>**Binge drinking**</u> is defined as 5 drinks <u>**within an hour**</u> for men and <u>**4**</u> drinks within an hour for women. **True.**

(Binge drinking on college campuses is most common in the freshman year – in the 18-25 age group.)

13. A <u>**heavy drinker**</u> is someone who drinks <u>**4-5**</u> drinks every night. **True***

14. All drinkers are <u>**drug users**</u>. **True.**

(Alcohol is defined as a drug by the AMA [American Medical Association] and the World Health Organization. It is a central nervous system depressant.)

15. <u>**Underage drinkers**</u> account for 25% of the alcohol consumed in the United States. **True.**

*Some students may dispute this because they come from cultures where drinking 4-5 drinks every night is common. This statistic also means that the 4-5 drinks is a regular habit over many years, not only drinking during college years.

Increasing Birth Size *page 104 (CD 2 TRACK 23)*

❀ Dictogloss

1. The percentage of babies that weigh at least 8 pounds, 8 ounces increased from 3 percent to 14 percent from 1970-1985.

2. In a land of king-size and super-size everything, big babies are generally taken as a sign of good health.

3. Big babies are stronger, healthier, and in possession of better immune systems.

4. We're getting too big and using up too many resources.

Note to teachers:

> 1 meter = 39.37 inches (or about 3 feet)
> 1 kilogram = 2.2 pounds

❀ Dictation

"**With regard to** evolution, we are in a **whole new ballgame**," said James Boster, an anthropologist at the University of Connecticut. "**Through most of human history** babies were born in primitive conditions. But **lots of women** died in childbirth. Now with access to **good medical care**, the previous consequences of having babies **that were too big** are remedied surgically.

In the last 200 years, growth has been dramatic. In 1760, Norwegian soldiers averaged **5 foot 3.** American soldiers drafted for World War I averaged **5 feet tall and 140 pounds**. Today the average Californian male is **5 feet 10 1/2** inches and weighs **188 pounds**.

What remains to be seen is how much larger people will grow. To project **how big humans may become**, anthropologists look to the past. **More than a million years ago** our African ancestors stood **about 6 feet tall**, according to Daniel Lieberman, a professor at Harvard University. But as early humans moved from a hunter-gatherer society to agriculture, food variety **decreased**, disease **increased**, and people migrated **to colder climates** —

favoring shorter, squatter physiques — and **as a result of** all these factors, heights shrank. It is only **in the last two centuries** that humans have begun to play catch-up. They haven't peaked yet, but they are getting close. In the Netherlands (**home to the tallest population in the world**) the average height of the men is **nearly 6 feet one inch**. It appears that genetics won't allow humans to get much bigger.

The difference between men and women, which has been shrinking **for thousands of years**, may some day disappear, anthropologists say. **Thousands of years ago** men were **30% taller than women**. Between 30,000 and 50,000 years ago, men and women grew noticeably **closer in size**. Today, height differences **average 7%**. The gender gap is directly related to mating habits, scientists say. The more polygamous a species, the greater the size differential between men and women.

Nutrition and Obesity *page 106 (CD 2 TRACK 24)*

❧ Dictation 1: Nutrition

1. Low-fat milk has more **calcium than whole** milk. **True.**

    (When fat is removed from milk, other nutrients, including calcium and phosphorus, become more concentrated. The healthiest choices are skim and 1 percent milk; 2 percent milk is not low-fat.)

2. Multivitamin pills can give you **extra energy**. **False.**

    (Vitamins don't provide energy (calories). Calories come from carbohydrates, proteins, fats, and alcohol.)

3. It's better to eat a **larger lunch** and a smaller dinner. **True.**

    (The calories consumed in a larger lunch get burned off more readily.)

4. People who do not eat meat, chicken, or fish are **not as healthy as** those who do. **False.**

    (Vegetarians who eat a balanced diet of protein, carbohydrates, and fat are just as healthy.)

5. Fresh vegetables are always **more nutritious than** frozen. **False.**

    (Fresh vegetables tend to lose their nutrients once they're picked, and the longer they sit, the more they lose. Frozen vegetables, if they're kept frozen, hold on to their vitamins.)

6. If you want to make one **change** in your diet, **cutting down** on fat would be better **than snacking** less often. **True.**

    (Experts agree that eating less fat is the key to a healthy diet.)

7. A glass or two of wine **or beer** will help you sleep well. **False.**

    (Drinking alcohol will allow you to get to sleep more easily, but sleep is often interrupted at 2 or 3 in the morning.)

8. **Laughter** helps keep you in good **condition**. **True.**

    (Your ability to find humor can prolong your life.)

9. When you're **on a diet**, it's better to drink white wine **than red**. **False.**

    (It makes no difference; so choose the wine you like. A 6-ounce glass of red or white wine contains about 130 calories.)

10. You've been asked to **serve the steak**. A good serving size would be **the same size as** a deck of cards. **True.**

    (For meat, fish, and poultry, the experts recommend a 3-ounce portion, about the size of a deck of cards. As a rule of thumb, a 4-ounce piece cooks down to 3 oz.)

11. Butter contains **more fat than margarine**.   **False..**

(A tablespoon of either butter or margarine contains 100 calories, every one of them from fat.)

12. Women who eat at least **5** servings of fruits and vegetables **daily** reduce their **risk** of diabetes by **40%**.   **True.**

❀ Dictation 2: Obesity

Despite a seeming obsession with their health, **diet**, and **exercise**, Americans are getting **fatter and fatter**. New information shows that more than half of all **adults** in the United States are **overweight**, and the number of obese people – defined **as being 30%** over the ideal weight – increased from **12%** in 1991 to **18%** in 1998.

Researchers say they are **stunned at** how fast Americans are **adding** extra pounds, and some say that **obesity** – which perhaps kills as many as **325,000 every year** – should be considered a real public health problem and not simply a **cosmetic** one.

Dr. George Blackburn, director of the division of **nutrition** at Beth Israel Deaconess Medical Center, said that **over the last** 15 years, Americans have become aware that diet and exercise can **reduce risk** for many health complications, such as high blood **pressure**, heart disease, or diabetes, but they just **aren't ready** to do it yet.

"Fewer people are doing what they know they should do. **Instead**, everybody just wants a **magic bullet**," Blackburn said. "But they don't **realize** if they can spend an extra few minutes **each day**, and as little as 200 **calories** less a day, they would be **20 pounds** lighter by the end of the year."

Two reasons why Americans are **gaining** weight are easy to **spot**:

• They **eat out** in restaurants at least **two or three** times a week.

• They **may join** a health club, but after **six** months **50%** of them quit.

Exercise *page 108 (CD 2 TRACK 25)*

❀ Dictogloss

1. If you do more exercise, your appetite will increase and keep you from losing weight. **False.**

   (This is a common misunderstanding. In fact, moderate physical exercise does not stimulate the appetite.)

2. Sports drinks can help you exercise more safely and effectively. **False.**

   (Sports drinks contain two main ingredients that are beneficial for exercise: sodium, which helps the body retain water, and sugar, which the body burns for energy. But very few people exercise enough to sweat away very much sodium or to use up their carbohydrate reserve, which the body converts to sugar. You'd have to jog for two hours to need a sports drink. What you need is lots of water.)

3. The more you sweat during exercise, the more fat you lose. **False.**

   (You lose no fat tissue through sweating, only fluid, which is replaced very quickly by normal thirst.)

4. Physical exercise is not necessary for losing weight. Dieting alone is enough. **True.**

   (But with diet alone, you lose muscle tissue as well as fat. When you exercise, as well, most of the weight loss is fat.)

5. Strength training tends to give women a bulky, masculine physique. **False.**

   (It's very difficult for women to build large muscles. That's because women have relatively low levels of the hormone testosterone, which influences muscle growth.)

❀ Dictation

Ruth Rothfarb of Cambridge was an **elderly athlete** who **inspired** many by **competing** in the Boston **Marathon** (26 miles), the Tufts 10K (10 kilometers), and other long-distance races. Mrs. Rothfarb, who **died** Wednesday at age **96,** began running at the age of **69**. She began running competitively a few years later.

She **competed** in several Boston **Marathons** and Tufts 10K races **as well as** long-distance races in Atlanta, Los Angeles, New Zealand, and Thailand before her retirement from **competitive** running at the age of **92**. She was born in Russia and **immigrated** to the United States as a teenager in **1913**. After her marriage, she **worked** full-time maintaining a home, raising two children, and helping her husband **run** the family clothing business.

At the age of **67** she found herself with **time on her hands** after her husband **died**, their business was sold, and her children were **grown**. "I had to do something," she said. "I wasn't going to sit around doing nothing."

She began taking walks **along** the Charles River and **around** Fresh Pond. When the jogging **craze** came to her neighborhood, she **picked** up her speed. "If they can do it, I can **too**." she said. "It's simple enough. All you have to do is pick up your feet and go."

In **1976**, she accompanied her son, Herbert, to a ten-kilometer race. "While everyone was **warming up,** I asked my son if they'd laugh at me if I ran," she said. "He said no. So I ran. And I finished. It took me a long time but I finished." She was **75** at the time.

At the age of **84** she was running about **10** miles a day and running **marathons** in about **5 1/2** hours. "I like to **get going**," she said. "If I feel like doing something, I want to do it. I don't have to wait around for anybody else. I don't believe in spending afternoons just sitting around having tea. I do things."

How's Your Mental Health? *page 110 (CD 2 TRACK 26)*

❀ Dictation

The Surgeon General of the United States recently **reported** that **one** in **five** Americans suffers from a **mental** illness. Although some may feel this is overstated, imagine that:

- **One** in **five** women will experience **clinical** depression in their lives, as will **one** in **seven** men.
- Eight to twelve percent of the population experiences a significant **anxiety disturbance**.
- **One** in **twenty** children has attention deficit hyperactivity disorder (ADHD).
- One percent of the population has **manic** depression or bipolar illness.
- **One** percent of the population has schizophrenia.

Through education and information it is important to be able to look at depression, anxiety, ADHD, and sleep **disorders** not as **weaknesses** but rather as real and medically based illnesses. Considering mental health problems to be **non-medically** based means that far too many will go unrecognized and **untreated**.

The **most common** mental illness is depression. Different forms of depression **range** from short-term, low mood after a **stressful** life experience to an **ongoing** form of depression linked to decreased energy, interest, **and concentration** along with changes in appetite and sleep — called **major depression**.

Depression may also take place in women following **childbirth** as well as in people during certain **seasons** of the year. Being unable to perform at work, having little wish to **socialize**, and becoming **distanced** from family members may all take place during depression. Depression very much needs to be viewed as a **medical** illness and not as a weakness. Recognizing and treating depression not only **enhances** life but also **saves** lives.

Note to teachers:

If this is a topic that your students would like to know more about and if your school has a psychology department, a professor may be willing to come and talk to the class, or perhaps someone from a counseling center can be interviewed by the class. You can also check out: www.askpsychmd.com/index.htm

AIDS *page 112 (CD 2 TRACK 27)*

❀ Dictogloss

1. Worldwide, 15-to-24-year-olds account for half of all new infections.

2. AIDS could kill nearly 70 million people worldwide over the next two decades.

3. People can have HIV without knowing that they have it because they don't have symptoms.

4. You can't tell by looking at someone whether she or he has HIV.

5. HIV can be passed from one person to another through blood, semen, or vaginal fluids.

Quiz

1. D 2. A 3. D 4. D

❀ Dictation

We tend to think of disease in simple terms: **infection** equals **illness.** It's a little different with HIV, since the virus can cause slow, subtle damage to the immune system **long before an infected person will feel ill**. Most health providers use the term "HIV disease" to identify the variety of changes **a person may experience** from initial infection to more advanced stages of serious life-threatening illness.

About 900,000 Americans are infected with AIDS, and a quarter of them do not know it, **according to** the CDC (US Centers for Disease Control and Prevention). **Another 25%** are not getting any kind of care for their disease. More than **400,000 people** are going **untreated** for HIV, and **they may be spreading it** through **unprotected sex** or **shared needles**.

Recent **data** suggests that **50,000 more people** are living with HIV or AIDS **than two years ago**. There is an estimated total **of between 850,000 and 950,000** currently living in the US with HIV infection. **Worldwide, 3 million people** die of AIDS every year and **40 million are infected**, most of them in Africa.

Recently Secretary of State Colin Powell, on an international MTV "town hall" show that reaches **375** million homes in **164** countries, said that while he respected the views of the church, "In my own judgment, **condoms are a way** to prevent infection, and, **therefore,**

I not only support their use, I encourage their use among young people who are sexually active and need to protect themselves."

In countries that **have gotten past taboos** and made greater use of condoms, the disease has been kept **in check**. In Brazil, a UN AIDS report in 2000 indicated that **87% of males** aged **16** to **25** with casual sex partners were using condoms with them, a much higher rate than in AIDS-affected countries. This, combined with a drug treatment program **that encourages testing** for HIV, has caused Brazil's infection rate **to plummet**.

The Immaculate Americans *page 115 (CD 2 TRACK 28)*

✿ Dictation

Body odor is **big business**. Every year, we immaculate Americans spend more money on **deodorants** and **mouthwashes** than we contribute to the United Way charity. In addition, we probably pass more time **scrubbing, washing**, spraying, bathing, **squirting**, and **gargling** than any other people in the history of the world. Every American, in fact, learns from **an early age** that cleanliness is next to Godliness – a sign that an individual is **morally pure** and **sinless**. No wonder that Americans spend more than **one billion dollars annually on soap** – it's part of our culture.

In other parts of the world, however, we **are regarded as** neurotically concerned with our **personal cleanliness**. In Europe, for example, Americans are **easily identified** by their demands for a room with a **private bath**. Meanwhile, their European **counterparts** usually stay in **less expensive rooms**, where they wash up daily in a small sink and take their **Saturday night baths** down the hall. In their own countries, anyone caught **showering** twice a day would probably **be regarded as** either eccentric or ill.

Americans can hardly take credit (**or blame**), however, for inventing a concern for cleanliness. Sniffing and **nose kissing** have long been practiced by Eskimos, Philippine Islanders, and Samoans, who **recognized the desire** for a pleasant odor. And bathing for purification is **an ancient custom** practiced by the early Hebrews, Muslims, and Hindus.

Plastics Alert *page 117 (CD 2 TRACK 29)*

To the teacher:

This is not a dictation but a reconstruction of a paragraph where students write the main idea in one sentence.

Possible directions (but do what you think will work for your students):

First listening: Let them listen only the first time.
Second listening: Take notes or just listen again.
Third listening (if necessary): Make sure they write something even if it's only a few words.

According to a recent news article, we should not be using plastic containers when heating our food in the microwave. This applies especially to foods that contain fat. Researchers say that the combination of fat, high heat, and plastics releases dioxins into the food and ultimately into the cells of the body. Because dioxins are highly toxic, doctors recommend using glass or ceramic containers for heating food.

Stem Cell Research *page 118 (CD 2 TRACK 30)*

❀ Dictation 1

In therapeutic cloning, **which seeks medical cures**, genetic material from a patient **is placed into** a hollowed-out egg, and then artificially stimulated to grow, creating an embryo genetically identical to the patient. **Researchers hope to extract stem cells** from these week-old embryos, then mold the flexible cells into easily used replacement tissue for patients. **But the process destroys the embryo**, ethically troubling many.

Scientists overwhelmingly oppose implanting cloned embryos in women **to produce babies, called reproductive cloning**. Several maverick researchers claim to have implanted women, **though no proof exists**. However, many mainstream scientists worry that such attempts could proliferate **as cloning becomes widespread** and researchers become more proficient.

❀ Dictation 2

Stacia Poulos has two cats, **and treasures them both**. But she'd never want **to double the pleasure** with either one of them.

"I'm not one for cloning. I'm not for it at all," the 23-year-old Scituate resident said **when asked her opinion** about researchers in Texas cloning a cat.

"It will lead **to human cloning**, and that is wrong. **It's one more step**. Sheep, and now this step," she said, as she prepared to get on a train at the Quincy Adams MBTA station this morning.

She said **cloning is wrong**, even if it means getting duplicates for Picky and Toledo, her two cats. "**I love them to death**, but I wouldn't clone them."

Jim Hyland, 33, of Braintree said, "**Leave life alone.** Cats shouldn't be cloned. Nobody should be cloned. They're spending **way too much money**, when they could be spending it on research for something useful: find a cure for AIDS or cancer." Hyland has a dog, a fox terrier named Max. "I love Max. He's 12 years old and I don't know what I would do if he died today. **But when his time is up, it's up**. Unfortunately, **that's life**."

Alternative Medicine *page 120 (CD 2 TRACK 31)*

❀ Dictation 1

<u>Not long ago</u>, the idea of treating pain with acupuncture or hypnosis would have **<u>raised many an eyebrow</u>** within the medical mainstream. **<u>But now a growing number of hospitals</u>** are offering patients alternative or complementary therapies **<u>combined with traditional medicine</u>**.

A big reason for the trend **<u>is consumer demand</u>**. A 1997 Harvard study reported **<u>that Americans made 629 million visits</u>** to alternative practitioners **<u>compared with 386 million visits</u>** to primary care doctors, spending $27 billion (a good part of it **<u>out of pocket)</u>** on alternative treatments.

Proponents say complementary techniques, particularly mind-body therapies, **<u>offer many benefits</u>**. They are non-invasive and have **<u>no side effects</u>**. And they tap into the healing power of the mind.

❀ Dictation 2

1. Complementary care uses variations of touch, **<u>from gentle stroking</u>** to deep tissue manipulation. The most common technique is **<u>Swedish massage</u>**, in which the muscles are stroked or kneaded **<u>with varying amounts of pressure.</u>**

2. A mind-body technique in which the patient **<u>becomes deeply relaxed;</u>** in this state the **<u>power of suggestion is used</u>** to ease symptoms of pain.

3. **<u>According to</u>** this ancient Chinese technique, **<u>each person has an energy force</u>** called Qi (pronounced chee), which travels through channels in the body. Pain or illness results when channels become blocked. To restore flow, **<u>fine needles are inserted</u>** at specific points on the **<u>skin's surface</u>**.

4. Complementary techniques include guided imagery, a form of self-hypnosis in which the patient visualizes positive images **<u>to ease pain</u>**; progressive muscle relaxation, in which the patient tenses, **<u>holds</u>**, and then **<u>releases</u>** muscle groups; and **<u>meditation</u>**, in which the patient **<u>tries to clear the mind</u>** by focusing on a **<u>word or sound</u>**.

5. A mind-body technique that uses sensors to measure physiological functions like muscle tension or gastrointestinal activity; **<u>as patients watch</u>** the "feedback" on a monitor, **<u>they become aware</u>** of how their bodies respond and learn how to control that response.

Matching

1. C - Massage Therapy   3. D - Acupuncture   5. E - Biofeedback
2. A - Hypnosis   4. B - Relaxation Therapy

A Smoking Issue *page 122 (CD 2 TRACK 32)*

❊ Dictation 1

College campuses are the latest battleground for **smokers** and **non-smokers**. Since **the turn of the century**, cities and towns throughout the nation have forced restaurants and bars **to go smoke-free**. In step with the times, colleges **across the country** have gone smoke-free or are considering the move. Recently Smith College **banned smoking in its dorms** and the University of Connecticut **followed suit**.

A 1999 study by the Harvard School of Public Health found that **27%** of non-commuter colleges and universities banned smoking everywhere — including **all residence halls** — while **55%** allowed it in residence halls.

For smokers' rights activists, the move **to ban smoking in college housing** is **just another step** in an anti-American drive to **discriminate against** and control a **segment of the population**. Barbara Aucoin, president of the Massachusetts chapter of Fight Ordinances and Restrictions to Control and Eliminate Smoking (FORCES), is **shocked by** smoking bans in college housing. She refers to **the recent rulings** of local health boards to ban smoking in bars and restaurants as "Nazi tactics."

"The **choice** to ban smoking **should be up to** the individual owners rather than the government," she said. "You take away that choice and we are not Americans anymore."

Kevin Kroner, Executive Director of Northeastern University's Tobacco Control Resource Center, said, "Your right to put these substances into your body should **extend as far as** your neighbor's lungs."

A research group for student affairs and institutional research conducted a survey of **927 residential students**. **A majority of the students**, smokers and non-smokers, said that smoking in private rooms **or designated areas** within some halls is the preferred policy.

❀ Dictation 2: Judge for Yourself

Vinny lived in an apartment **that was directly above** that of a woman who was a cigarette smoker. He filed a nuisance suit against her, claiming **that the smoke came up** through vents and cracks **and was driving him crazy**. The woman did not believe **that smoking in her own home** was an illegal activity. She told the judge **the six cigarettes she smoked a day** did not qualify as a nuisance and cited the fact that there was no mention of **smoking being illegal in the lease**.

❀ The Verdict

The judge **ruled against** Vinny, ruling that the smoke **from a few cigarettes a day** was **not a significant enough annoyance**.

Other books from Pro Lingua

AT THE INTERMEDIATE AND ADVANCED LEVELS

Discussion Strategies — Carefully structured pair and small group work at the advanced-intermediate level. Excellent preparation for students who will participate in academic or professional work that requires effective participation in discussion and seminars.

Conversation Strategies — 24 structured pair activities for developing strategic conversation skills at the intermediate level. Students learn the words, phrases, and conventions used by native speakers in active, give-and-take, everyday conversation.

Writing Strategies: A Student-Centered Approach — Two texts jam-packed with writing activities. Each covers four modes of writing. Book One *(Advanced Intermediate)* teaches • Description, • Narration, • Exposition, and • Comparison and Contrast. Book Two *(Advanced)* covers • Process, • Cause and Effect, • Extended Definition, and • Argumentation. Coordinated with these lessons are Fluency Writing Exercises and lessons on Grammar Problems and Terminology.

Write for You — A teacher resource book with copyable handouts. The focus is on creative activities that lead to effective writing by intermediate students who are intending to further their education.

Pearls of Wisdom — At the heart of this integrated skills builder are twelve stories from Africa and the Caribbean, collected and told by Dr. Raouf Mama of Benin. Student text for reading/listening, workbook for discussion/vocabulary building, two cassettes.

The Modal Book – 14 units explore the form, meaning, and use of the American English modal verb system, one semantic grouping at a time.

A Phrasal Verb Affair – over 200 phrasal verbs are presented and practiced in the context of a 15-episode soap opera. A dramatic reading on CD is available.

Shenanigames — Grammar-focused, interactive ESL activities and games providing practice with a full range of grammar structures. Photocopyable.

Getting a Fix on Vocabulary — A student text and workbook that focuses on affixation—building words by adding prefixes and suffixes to a root.

Lexicarry — Pictures for Learning Languages the Active Way. Over 4500 everyday words and expressions in 192 contexts that make conversation and interactive learning easy. There is a special new section on proverbs and sayings. Lots of words, even for very advanced students. Additional material at www.Lexicarry.com.

Nobel Prize Winners — 18 brief biographies for listening and/or reading. All the reading passages are also available as gapped exercises for reading or dictation. Text and three cassettes.

Web Store: www.ProLinguaAssociates.com